I0411856

August 2014

BUREAU OF PRISONS

Management of New Prison Activations Can Be Improved

GAO Highlights

Highlights of GAO-14-709, a report to congressional requesters

BUREAU OF PRISONS

Management of New Prison Activations Can Be Improved

Why GAO Did This Study

The federal inmate population has increased over the last two decades, and as of July 2014, BOP was responsible for the custody and care of more than 216,000 inmates. To handle the projected growth of between 2,500 and 3,000 or more inmates per year from 2015 through 2020, BOP has spent about $1.3 billion constructing five new institutions and acquiring one in Thomson, Illinois. BOP is activating these institutions by staffing and equipping them and populating them with inmates.

GAO was requested to review BOP's activation process of newly constructed and acquired institutions. GAO reviewed, among other things, (1) the extent to which BOP is activating institutions within estimated timeframes and has an activation policy or schedules that meet best practices, and (2) why DOJ purchased Thomson and how the purchase affected system wide costs. GAO reviewed BOP budget documents from fiscal years 2008 to 2015 and assessed schedules against GAO's *Schedule Assessment Guide*. GAO conducted site visits to the six institutions, interviewed BOP officials, and reviewed staffing data from fiscal years 2010 through 2013.

What GAO Recommends

GAO recommends that DOJ use its annual budget justification to communicate to Congress factors that might delay prison activation, and that BOP analyze institution-level staffing data and develop and implement a comprehensive activation policy and a schedule that reflects best practices. DOJ concurred with all of GAO's recommendations.

View GAO-14-709. For more information, contact Dave Maurer at (202) 512-9627 or maurerd@gao.gov.

What GAO Found

The Department of Justice's (DOJ) Federal Bureau of Prisons (BOP) is behind schedule activating all six new institutions—the process by which it prepares them for inmates—and does not have a policy to guide activation or an activation schedule that reflects best practices. BOP is behind schedule, in part, because of challenges, such as staffing, posed by the locations of the activating institutions. According to BOP officials, delays in receiving congressionally directed activation funding can exacerbate these challenges (see fig.). None of the six institutions is fully activated, or at rated capacity, as they do not house the number of inmates they are designed to safely and securely house.

Schedule Slippages for Institutions in the Activation Process

Source: GAO analysis of Bureau of Prisons budget documents. | GAO-14-709

BOP does not effectively communicate to Congress how the locations of new institutions may affect activation schedules. BOP officials said that when directed by Congress to investigate a location, they consider this as direction to focus on construction at that site. DOJ and BOP could more effectively manage activation timelines and costs by using the BOP annual budget justification to communicate to Congress the factors associated with certain locations that can delay activations, such as challenges hiring staff and placing inmates in institutions. Also, BOP officials said they review staffing data system-wide, but they have not prioritized an analysis of such data at the institution level. Analyzing staffing data on institutions in the activation process could help BOP assess its progress in staffing and tailoring effective mitigating strategies. Finally, BOP lacks a comprehensive activation policy to guide activations, as well as an activation schedule that reflects best practices, and it has largely relied on staff's past experience to complete ongoing activations. Developing and implementing a comprehensive policy and a schedule that reflects best practices, could better position BOP to meet its estimated timeframes and activation costs.

DOJ purchased Thomson to help reduce crowding among inmates requiring high levels of security. Once it is fully populated, it will reduce BOP-wide crowding by 16 percent at the high-security level. Thomson will cost about $160 million annually to operate once fully activated, adding to BOP's system-wide costs. BOP officials said Thomson will provide benefits, such as high-security bed space, which outweigh the costs associated with the institution.

Contents

Figures

Abbreviations

ADX	Administrative Maximum
B&F	Buildings and Facilities
DOJ	Department of Justice
EHRI	Enterprise Human Resources Integration
BOP	Federal Bureau of Prisons
FCI	Federal Correctional Institution
M&R	Modernization and Repair
OPM	Office of Personnel Management
S&E	Salaries and Expenses
USP	U.S. Penitentiary

GAO

U.S. GOVERNMENT ACCOUNTABILITY OFFICE

441 G St. N.W.
Washington, DC 20548

August 22, 2014

Congressional Requesters

The Department of Justice's (DOJ) Federal Bureau of Prisons (BOP) requested about $6.9 billion in fiscal year 2014 to provide for the custody and care of an inmate population that has increased from about 24,000 in fiscal year 1980 to over 216,000 in July 2014. According to DOJ, as of July 2014, BOP-operated institutions are about 31 percent overcrowded, which occurs when institutions house more inmates than they are designed to hold. Moreover, according to BOP's most recent long-range capacity plan included in DOJ's annual congressional budget justification for BOP, the bureau projects annual inmate growth of between 2,500 and 3,000 or more from fiscal years 2015 through 2020.[1] BOP is not responsible for controlling the flow of inmates into the federal prison system, as convicted felons are placed directly into BOP's custody and care, but BOP is responsible for confining these inmates safely and securely. As we reported in September 2012, this responsibility can be challenging with a growing inmate population.[2] In particular, we found that crowding has negatively affected inmates housed in BOP institutions, institutional staff, and the infrastructure of BOP facilities, and has contributed to inmate misconduct, which affects staff and inmate security and safety. In recognition of the difficulties crowding causes, DOJ's Inspector General included detention and incarceration among DOJ's top 10 management and performance challenges department-wide for 2013, and noted that the department has identified crowding as a material weakness every year since 2006.

BOP considers reducing crowding rates system-wide to be a strategic goal and has spent over $1.3 billion on the construction and acquisition of six new federal institutions to help alleviate crowding across the prison system. Specifically, BOP constructed five federal prisons: (1) Federal Correctional Institution (FCI) Aliceville in Alabama, (2) FCI Berlin in New Hampshire, (3) FCI Hazelton in West Virginia, (4) FCI Mendota in

---

[1]For the purposes of our report, we refer to DOJ's annual congressional budget justifications for BOP as BOP's budget justifications.

[2]GAO, *Bureau of Prisons: Growing Inmate Crowding Negatively Affects Inmates, Staff, and Infrastructure,* GAO-12-743 (Washington, D.C.: Sept. 12, 2012).

California, and (5) U.S. Penitentiary (USP) Yazoo City in Mississippi.[3] In addition, BOP acquired the Thomson Correctional Center, now referred to as Administrative USP Thomson, from the state of Illinois in October 2012 to address crowding for inmates requiring high levels of security.[4] BOP is currently working to activate these institutions—a process by which BOP staffs and equips institutions, and populates them with inmates—and has received or is waiting for congressionally directed funding to activate all six of these new institutions.[5] In addition to BOP, DOJ is also working to address the growth in the prison population, and in 2013, launched its Smart on Crime Initiative, which includes several efforts to modernize the criminal justice system, including reprioritizing federal law enforcement prosecutions to focus on the most serious cases. Additionally, over the past 2 years, Members of Congress have introduced at least five bills to date that seek to modify federal sentencing requirements in order to reduce the length of incarceration of inmates convicted of nonviolent drug-related offenses.

In light of crowding conditions and BOP's recent construction of new institutions and the acquisition of the Thomson Correctional Center, you asked us to review BOP's activation process. Specifically, this report addresses the following questions:

1. To what extent has BOP activated the six institutions within estimated time frames, and to what extent does BOP have an activation policy or schedules that meet best practices?

2. How has BOP covered the costs of maintaining the six institutions?

---

[3]BOP has several types of institutions, including FCIs that generally house inmates who need less security than those housed in USPs, which generally house inmates requiring higher security.

[4]According to BOP officials, Administrative USP Thomson may hold both high-security and maximum-security inmates, but BOP is still in the process of determining the specific types of inmates that the institution will house.

[5]Generally, either the annual appropriation act or the conference report accompanying BOP's annual appropriation act directs BOP to use Salaries and Expenses (S&E) appropriations for activation activities at particular institutions. Conference report language that is incorporated by reference into an appropriations act becomes part of the public law. However, BOP generally follows directives contained in the conference report language even if not incorporated into the appropriations act. For the purpose of this report, we refer to the conference report language as "congressional direction" and the related funding as "congressionally directed activation funding."

GAO-14-709 Bureau of Prisons

3. How will the addition of each institution likely affect system-wide crowding rates?

4. Why did DOJ purchase the Thomson Correctional Center, and how, if at all, will it affect costs?

To determine whether BOP has activated the six institutions within estimated time frames, we reviewed documents that accompany BOP's annual congressional budget justifications, called budget exhibits, from fiscal years 2008 through 2014 that include timelines for when BOP expects to activate new institutions.[6] We also analyzed data from the Office of Personnel Management's (OPM) human resources database, Enterprise Human Resources Integration (EHRI) Statistical Data Mart, for fiscal years 2010 through 2013 to determine the extent to which staffing challenges identified by institutions in the activation process affected BOP's ability to meet estimated time frames related to activation.[7] Further, we reviewed legislation enacted from relevant fiscal years, specifically fiscal years 1999 through 2006, and associated reports to identify the process through which specific institution locations are identified, as well as BOP's assessments of proposed locations for new institutions. Additionally, we evaluated the extent to which BOP's schedule documents used for completing activation for each institution complied with and reflected best practices outlined in GAO's *Schedule Assessment Guide*.[8] We also interviewed agency officials on the challenges, if any, institutions face related to activation and the actions BOP has taken to mitigate the effects of those challenges.

---

[6]BOP was unable to provide full budget justifications prior to fiscal year 2008.

[7]OPM's EHRI is a collection of human resources, payroll, and training data that facilitates management of personnel in the federal government. We used EHRI data to report hires and separations through the end of each relevant fiscal year. To report the most current data on hires and separations in fiscal year 2014—from October, 2013 through July, 2014—we relied on BOP to provide this information from its personnel database. We determined that BOP's staffing data are comparable to our analysis of OPM's EHRI data and are reliable for the purposes of our report.

[8]GAO, *GAO Schedule Assessment Guide: Best Practices for Project Schedules*, GAO-12-120G (Washington, D.C.: May 2012). Our *Schedule Assessment Guide* provides guidance to agencies on developing and maintaining reliable, high-quality schedules to manage programs and projects, such as construction or activation projects. We developed this guide through a compilation of best practices that federal cost-estimating organizations and industry use.

To determine how BOP has covered the costs of maintaining the six institutions while waiting for congressional direction on activation funding, we reviewed BOP's annual congressional budget justifications from fiscal years 2008 through 2015. We also reviewed BOP's annual spend plans, which DOJ or its components develop after receiving an appropriation, for fiscal years 2010 through 2014 to identify congressionally directed activation funding. Further, we analyzed data on actual obligations BOP made from fiscal years 2010, or the first year BOP made activation-related obligations for those six institutions, through March 2014 to fund and activate the six institutions to determine the total cost of new institution activations. We also reviewed program statements, which are BOP's formal policies and procedures, related to using appropriated funds for building projects.

To determine how each new institution will likely affect system-wide crowding rates, we evaluated BOP's long-range capacity plan that accompanied BOP's fiscal year 2015 congressional budget justification. That plan includes BOP's estimates of the future inmate population and crowding rates through fiscal year 2020, and assumes that all six institutions in our review will be fully populated, or fully activated, by fiscal year 2016. We then used data in that plan to calculate estimated crowding rates—assuming the new institutions were not fully activated by fiscal year 2016 (e.g., did not provide any beds)—by subtracting the number of beds the six institutions would otherwise have added to overall capacity in that fiscal year. Our analysis compared crowding rates with and without the addition of new beds provided by the six institutions and examined the effect of that additional capacity across (1) all BOP institutions, (2) respective security levels of each institution, and (3) gender.

To assess why DOJ purchased the Thomson Correctional Center in 2012, we reviewed BOP's congressional budget justifications and accompanying budget exhibits that specifically requested funds for Thomson from fiscal years 2011 through 2015; state of Illinois documents on selling the Thomson Correctional Center to the federal government that were produced in 2010; and relevant acquisition documents, such as an environmental assessment and appraisals of the institution. We also reviewed relevant statutes to understand the department's legal authority to acquire the Thomson Correctional Center. To determine how, if at all, the purchase of Thomson affected costs, we reviewed BOP's

Modernization and Repair Unfunded Priorities list from 2012, which was the list available when DOJ purchased Thomson.[9] We also analyzed BOP budget documentation to determine how much BOP will spend to operate the institution once it is fully activated.

To address all of the objectives in our review, we conducted site visits to all six institutions, and interviewed institution and regional office staff about the challenges, if any, they face during activation.[10] We also interviewed BOP officials to discuss crowding, cost and schedule estimates, and any potential cost implications of the Thomson purchase. To assess the reliability of data related to BOP's staffing, obligations, and the inmate population, we reviewed documentation related to BOP's staffing database; annual congressional budget requests; and the Sentry database, which contains inmate population data.[11] We interviewed human resources officials from BOP's Central Office to discuss what data BOP provides to OPM to verify our data analysis and tested the data for missing data, outliers, and obvious errors to ensure that the data are reliable. We also conducted interviews with knowledgeable agency officials about related internal controls of databases. We determined that the data used as a basis for these findings are reliable for the purposes of our report.

We conducted this performance audit from November 2013 to August 2014 in accordance with generally accepted government auditing standards. Those standards require that we plan and perform the audit to obtain sufficient, appropriate evidence to provide a reasonable basis for

---

[9]BOP uses funds for modernization and repair activities to cover the costs of items on this list. BOP designates modernization and repair funds, which are aimed at rehabilitating, modernizing, and renovating buildings and associated systems, as well as repairing or replacing utilities or other critical infrastructure at BOP institutions. Because DOJ acquired, rather than constructed, the Thomson Correctional Center, we analyzed the extent to which purchasing the Thomson Correctional Center affected other BOP costs.

[10]BOP has six regional offices, each led by a regional director, covering the North Central, Northeast, South Central, Mid-Atlantic, Southeast, and Western regions of the United States. BOP's regional offices and its Central Office, which has its headquarters in Washington, D.C., provide administrative oversight and support to prisons, among other things. We interviewed officials from the regional offices that have oversight of the prisons undergoing activation in our review, which include all but the South Central region.

[11]BOP's Sentry database is an information system containing, among other things, information related to the care, classification, subsistence, protection, discipline, and programs of federal inmates.

our findings and conclusions based on our audit objectives. We believe that the evidence obtained provides a reasonable basis for our findings and conclusions based on our audit objectives.

Background

Federal Prison System

To carry out its responsibility for the custody and care of federal offenders, BOP currently houses inmates across six geographic regions in 120 long-term federal institutions.[12] The Central Office and regional offices provide administrative oversight and support to institutions, among other things. The management officials located at each institution, including wardens and associate wardens, provide overall direction and implement policies.

Male long-term institutions include four security-level designations— minimum, low, medium, and high—and female long-term institutions include three security designations—minimum, low, and high. The security-level designation of a facility depends on the level of security and staff supervision that the facility is able to provide, such as the presence of security towers; perimeter barriers; the type of inmate housing, including dormitory, cubicle, or cell-type housing; and inmate-to-staff ratio. Additionally, BOP designates some of its institutions as administrative institutions, which specifically serve inmates awaiting trial, or those with intensive medical or mental health conditions, regardless of the level of supervision these inmates require. As of June 2014, BOP owned and operated seven stand-alone minimum-security institutions, 30 low-security institutions, 47 medium-security institutions, 16 high-security institutions, 1 administrative maximum (ADX) institution that houses inmates requiring the highest levels of security, and 19 administrative institutions. Many of these facilities are colocated on BOP-operated complexes that also contain minimum-security camps, which are

---

[12]In addition to these long-term federal institutions, BOP also houses inmates in privately managed facilities and home detention. According to BOP officials, privately managed contract facilities are low security and primarily house non-U.S. citizens convicted of crimes while in this country legally or illegally. Home detention describes all circumstances under which an inmate is serving a portion of his or her sentence while residing in his or her home. BOP also houses inmates in 200 residential reentry centers, and BOP officials stated that they use an additional 49 residential reentry centers through intergovernmental agreements for work release purposes.

nonsecure facilities that generally house nonviolent, low-risk offenders that are not included in this count. For example, USP Yazoo City is located on the Yazoo City Complex, which also includes a medium-security FCI, a low-security FCI, and a minimum-security camp.

BOP calculates the number of inmates a given institution is built to safely and securely house and defines this as its rated capacity. BOP establishes a rated capacity for each of the institutions that it owns and operates. In determining rated capacity, BOP considers occupancy and space requirements. According to BOP, rated capacity is the basis for measuring crowding and is essential to both managing the inmate population and BOP's annual congressional budget justifications for resources.

After an inmate receives his or her sentence, BOP initially designates that person to a particular institution based on (1) the level of security and supervision the inmate requires; (2) the level of security and staff supervision the institution is able to provide; (3) the inmate's program needs, such as residential drug treatment or intensive medical care; (4) where the inmate resides at the time of sentencing; (5) the level of crowding in an institution; and (6) any additional security measures to ensure the protection of victims, witnesses, and the public.[13]

BOP's Schedule Estimates

BOP communicates its schedule estimates related to activating new institutions to Congress through the annual budget process. BOP receives appropriated funds through two accounts—Buildings and Facilities (B&F) and Salaries and Expenses (S&E)—which BOP has divided into subaccounts, called decision units. The B&F account funds the construction of new institutions and the maintenance of existing institutions. Specifically, the B&F account has two subaccounts: (1) new construction and (2) modernization and repair. The B&F account includes no-year appropriations, which are available until expended. BOP's B&F account's modernization and repair subaccount funds are used to rehabilitate, modernize, and renovate buildings and associated systems, as well as repair or replace utilities or other critical infrastructure at BOP institutions. BOP's B&F budget justification includes accompanying

---

[13]BOP, *Inmate Security Designation and Custody Classification,* Program Statement P5100.08 (Washington, D.C.: Sept. 12, 2006).

budget exhibits, which, among other things, provide estimated timelines for when new institutions will provide rated capacity. Broadly, the S&E account covers costs for staffing; inmate medical care, food, and programming; and utilities at existing institutions. Specifically, the S&E account has four subaccounts: (1) inmate care and programs, (2) institution security and administration, (3) contract confinement, and (4) management and administration. Generally, the S&E account includes 1-year appropriations, which are available for obligation only in the fiscal year for which they were appropriated.

Description of the Activation Process

BOP receives congressionally directed funding for activation—the overall process by which BOP staffs and equips institutions and then populates them with inmates—through its S&E account.[14] BOP officials stated that, generally, BOP does not start the activation process until it has received congressionally directed activation funding. Upon receipt of congressionally directed activation funds, BOP begins completing what, for the purposes of this report, we consider "preactivation" steps, which include completing renovations; hiring staff, such as wardens and executive staff to manage the institution; and ordering supplies and equipment. Preactivation also includes meeting with community members, recruiting and training new staff, and furnishing the new institution.

When these steps are completed, the institution begins receiving inmates, and when this occurs, for the purposes of this report, we consider that institution to be partially activated. Once the institution houses inmates at

---

[14]The annual appropriations act or the conference report accompanying BOP's annual appropriations act may direct BOP to use S&E appropriations for activation activities at particular institutions. For example, the Consolidated and Further Continuing Appropriations Act, 2013, Pub. L. No. 113-6, 127 Stat. 198, 249, stated "[t]hat of the amount provided [for Salaries and Expenses] . . . not less than $99,496,000 shall be for activation of newly constructed prisons in Berlin, New Hampshire, Aliceville, Alabama, Yazoo City, Mississippi, and Hazelton, West Virginia, as requested in the Department's fiscal year 2013 budget." As another example, the conference report, H.R. Con. Rep. No. 111-366, at 671 (2009), accompanying the Consolidated Appropriations Act, 2010, Pub. L. No. 111-117, 123 Stat. 3034 (2009), directed that "[o]f the total amount provided,[for Salaries and Expenses] . . . not less than $22,000,000 shall be used for the activation of FCI Mendota." Conference report language that is incorporated by reference into the appropriations act becomes part of the public law. However, according to BOP officials, BOP generally follows directives contained in conference report language even if not incorporated into the appropriations act.

its rated capacity, or the number of inmates BOP determines the institution can safely and securely house, we consider that institution to be fully activated. All of the institutions in our review are currently in the preactivation or partial activation phases of the activation process because they do not yet house the number of inmates they were designed to hold. See figure 1 for a description of the life cycle of those institutions.

Figure 1: Life Cycle of Federal Bureau of Prisons' (BOP) Institutions

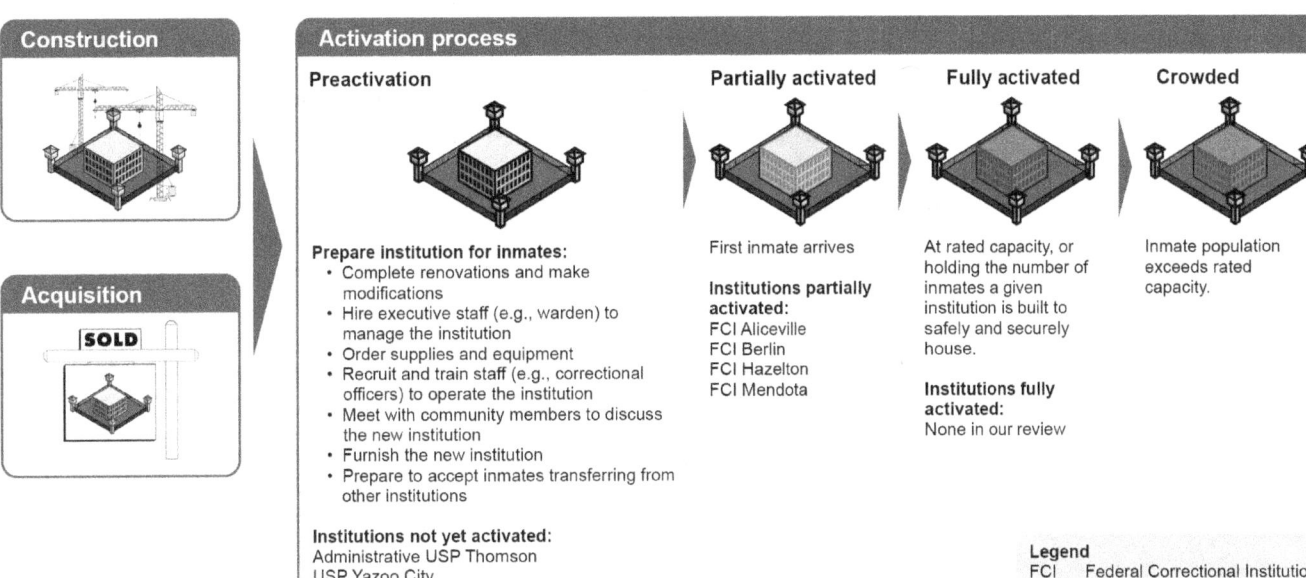

BOP's Design and Construction Branch is responsible for, among other things, overseeing the construction of new institutions, and when construction of an institution is almost complete, it transfers responsibility to the regional office or the local institution, thereby formally transitioning from construction to the beginning of the activation process. Once this responsibility has been transferred, regional or local officials work with the construction contractor to ensure that all items covered by the construction contractor's warranty, such as cooling and heating systems, are working properly prior to the warranty's expiration. They also work to conduct some alterations, installations, and repairs, such as placing additional razor wire and upgrading security features, that must be completed before the institution can securely house inmates. BOP made similar repairs to four of the six institutions in our review.

When the institution is ready to accept inmates, BOP issues an "Activation Memo" that specifies the criteria that inmates must meet in order to be housed in the new institution. Such criteria are based on the security level of the institution and the medical and mental health care services the institution was designed to provide. The criteria also generally include inmate characteristics that will allow for smooth transitions as the institution prepares for activation. For example, the Activation Memo may state that inmates should have histories of good conduct, no prior gang affiliation, and be generally healthy. Institutions that have inmates that meet those criteria can request that those inmates be transferred to the activating institution by submitting a formal request to the Designation and Sentence Computation Center, which officially approves the transfer. The Designation and Sentence Computation Center is also responsible for classifying inmate security levels and designating those inmates to specific institutions.

Background on Institutions in the Activation Process

From fiscal years 2005 through 2007, the President's annual budget request included a moratorium on new institution construction in an effort to have BOP take greater advantage of public and private sector bed space, which operate under contract with BOP, to meet the need for greater capacity. As a result of that moratorium, BOP officials reported that they were reluctant to proceed with the construction of several institutions, as we previously reported.[15] BOP has six federal institutions across the country currently in different phases of the activation process, as we discuss later in this report. See figure 2 for a description of each of those institutions.

---

[15]GAO, *Prison Construction: Clear Communication on the Accuracy of Cost Estimates and Project Changes Is Needed*, GAO-08-634 (Washington, D.C.: May 29, 2008). In that report, we recommended that the Attorney General of the United States instruct the Director of BOP to clearly communicate in DOJ's annual congressional budget submission (1) the extent to which project costs may vary from initial estimates and (2) changes that may affect the functionality of projects. BOP agreed with and implemented our recommendation.

Figure 2: Map of Federal Bureau of Prisons' (BOP) Institutions in the Activation Process

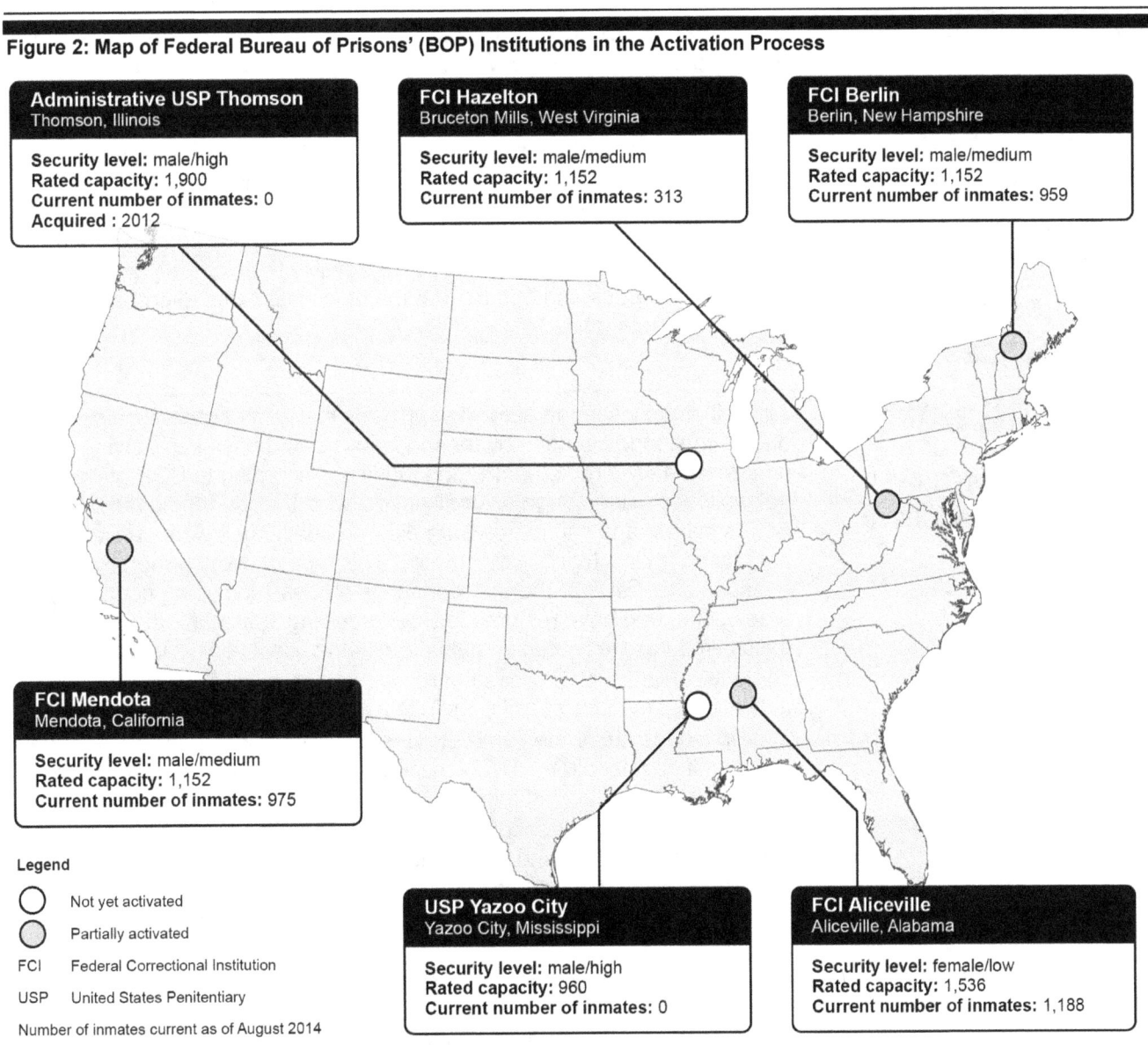

Administrative USP Thomson
Thomson, Illinois

Security level: male/high
Rated capacity: 1,900
Current number of inmates: 0
Acquired : 2012

FCI Hazelton
Bruceton Mills, West Virginia

Security level: male/medium
Rated capacity: 1,152
Current number of inmates: 313

FCI Berlin
Berlin, New Hampshire

Security level: male/medium
Rated capacity: 1,152
Current number of inmates: 959

FCI Mendota
Mendota, California

Security level: male/medium
Rated capacity: 1,152
Current number of inmates: 975

Legend

◯ Not yet activated
◑ Partially activated
FCI Federal Correctional Institution
USP United States Penitentiary

Number of inmates current as of August 2014

USP Yazoo City
Yazoo City, Mississippi

Security level: male/high
Rated capacity: 960
Current number of inmates: 0

FCI Aliceville
Aliceville, Alabama

Security level: female/low
Rated capacity: 1,536
Current number of inmates: 1,188

Source: GAO analysis of Bureau of Prisons documents; Map Resources (map). | GAO-14-709

BOP Is behind Schedule Fully Activating New Institutions, and Does Not Have an Activation Policy or Schedules That Meet Best Practices

BOP is behind schedule in fully activating, or reaching rated capacity for, all six institutions in the activation process. This is due, in part, to challenges posed by the locations of the activating institutions. However, although the institutions' locations posed challenges related to staffing, BOP is not effectively monitoring staffing challenges at individual institutions to ensure that they are staffed and, in turn, fully activated, within estimated time frames. Further, BOP does not have a policy in place to guide the activation process, or an associated schedule that meets best practices, which limits BOP's ability to accurately assess activation progress and ensure that the new institutions effectively reduce crowding as intended.

BOP Is behind Schedule, In Part, because of Challenges Posed by Institutions' Locations

All six institutions in the activation process have had schedule slippages due to challenges caused by their locations and delays in receiving congressionally directed activation funding. According to BOP officials, delays in receiving congressionally directed activation funding are outside BOP's control and can exacerbate existing challenges with staffing or populating an institution with inmates. This type of delay generally occurs because of aspects of the appropriations process, including continuing resolutions, that have resulted in BOP receiving its final funding level and associated congressional direction late in the fiscal year.[16] In addition, in some fiscal years, BOP does not receive congressionally directed activation funding for specific institutions.[17] Generally, either the annual appropriations act or the conference report accompanying BOP's annual appropriations act directs BOP to use S&E appropriations for activation activities at particular institutions.[18] BOP generally follows directives contained in the conference report language even if not incorporated into the appropriations act and therefore, in practice, does not activate institutions without congressional direction. Figure 3 illustrates the fiscal year in which BOP initially expected each institution to be fully activated,

---

[16]Continuing resolutions provide funding when action on regular appropriation bills is not completed before the beginning of the fiscal year. GAO, *A Glossary of Terms Used in the Federal Budget Process*, GAO-05-734SP (Washington, D.C.: September 2005).

[17]For the purpose of this report, we refer to the conference report language as "congressional direction" and the related funding as "congressionally directed activation funding."

[18]Broadly, the S&E account covers costs for staffing; inmate medical care, food, and programming; and utilities at existing institutions.

the subsequent revisions to that estimate, and the reasons for delay. Appendix I provides additional details on how delays in congressionally directed activation funding have resulted in schedule slippages for each of the institutions in the activation process.

Figure 3: Schedule Slippages for Federal Bureau of Prisons' (BOP) Institutions in the Activation Process

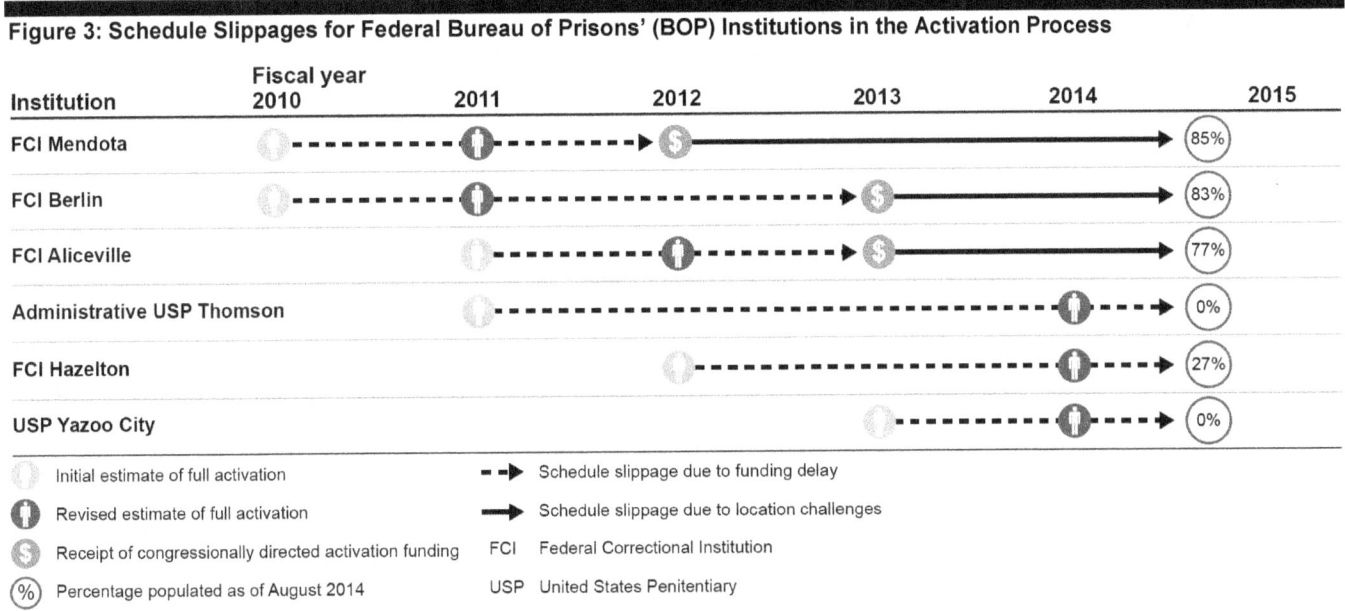

Initial estimate of full activation		Schedule slippage due to funding delay
Revised estimate of full activation		Schedule slippage due to location challenges
Receipt of congressionally directed activation funding	FCI	Federal Correctional Institution
Percentage populated as of August 2014	USP	United States Penitentiary

Source: GAO analysis of Bureau of Prisons budget documents. | GAO-14-709

Note: Activation is the overall process by which BOP staffs and equips institutions and then populates them with inmates. Once the institution houses inmates at its rated capacity, or the number of inmates BOP determines the institution can safely and securely house, we consider that institution to be fully activated. BOP officials stated that, generally, BOP does not start the activation process until it has received congressionally directed activation funding. Generally, either the annual appropriation act or the conference report accompanying BOP's annual appropriation act directs BOP to use Salaries and Expenses (S&E) appropriations for activation activities at particular institutions. Conference report language that is incorporated by reference into an appropriations act becomes part of the public law. However, BOP generally follows directives contained in the conference report language even if not incorporated into the appropriations act. For the purpose of this report, we refer to the conference report language as "congressional direction" and the related funding as "congressionally directed activation funding."

On our site visits to these institutions, we found that the locations of these institutions posed challenges related to staffing institutions and populating them with inmates within schedule estimates. For example, officials from FCI Aliceville stated that the institution's location made it challenging to hire staff up to authorized staffing levels during activation because of the low locality pay in Alabama compared with pay in other states.[19] According to officials, it has been difficult to find local applicants who could pass BOP's preemployment background check because prospective hires often had disqualifying levels of debt, even though they met the qualifications based on skill.[20] Similarly, officials from the Southeastern Regional Office stated that staffing two of the institutions within its region—FCI Aliceville and USP Yazoo City—has been challenging because of their rural locations. Further, officials from USP Yazoo City told us that it was particularly challenging to hire medical staff because of the institution's location and low pay in that area.

Moreover, we found on our site visits that the locations of some of these institutions also posed challenges related to populating them with inmates. In particular, these institutions generally accept inmates who are healthy, because the institutions are not located close to hospitals that can provide care for inmates with chronic or serious conditions requiring frequent visits, such as those with liver disease.[21] For example, officials from FCI Berlin told us that they had difficulty populating the institution with inmates because it could provide care only for generally healthy inmates, given its distance from major hospitals.[22] In fact, FCI Berlin is more than 2 hours away from the closest large hospital that can provide care for inmates with serious health conditions. As a result, according to officials from FCI Berlin, they originally planned to transfer to FCI Berlin only those inmates who are in overall stable health—those with a Care Level 1 designation—as doing so would minimize the need to regularly

[19]BOP determines the number of staff a new institution is authorized to hire based on funding levels and security levels of the new institution. Each activating institution is authorized to hire up to a certain number of staff, from within BOP or from outside the agency, including applicants from the local community. Hiring is generally funded through congressionally directed activation funding.

[20]BOP's preemployment check assesses applicants' financial and criminal histories to ensure that they are not vulnerable to corruption within the institution.

[21]BOP determines the level of medical care for a new institution based on the types of medical care services available in the local area. BOP-operated institutions generally provide a range of outpatient services related to primary health care and transport inmates with medical emergencies to the nearest hospital.

[22]FCI Berlin was not designed to provide acute or intensive medical care services at the institution.

transport inmates to faraway hospitals for necessary medical care.[23] However, there were not enough Care Level 1 inmates who also met the other criteria FCI Berlin specified, such as inmate security level, so the institution expanded its health care designation to also accept stable Care Level 2 inmates, who need more medical care than Care Level 1 inmates. BOP officials acknowledged that distance from major hospitals is a primary factor in determining the care level for institutions, such as FCI Berlin.

Although the specific locations of these new institutions can delay activation, BOP does not communicate to Congress the effect that location can have on BOP's ability to fully activate the institutions and to do so within estimated time frames. Our analysis of legislation enacted from fiscal years 1999 through 2006 and associated reports shows that conference reports directed BOP to investigate specific locations to determine whether institutions could be built there and to identify land where the institutions would eventually be built. In some cases, such as for FCI Berlin, the conference report accompanying DOJ's annual appropriations act for fiscal year 2002 directed BOP to begin partial site selection and planning for an institution to be located in Berlin, New Hampshire.[24] In contrast, for USP Yazoo City, the conference report accompanying DOJ's annual appropriations act for fiscal year 2000 directed BOP to study the feasibility of constructing an institution in Yazoo City, Mississippi.[25] In response to congressional direction to investigate a given location, BOP conducts environmental assessments or

---

[23]BOP classifies inmates into four categories of medical care needs, ranging from Care Level 1, which includes generally healthy inmates, to Care Level 4, which includes inmates with the most serious medical conditions. According to BOP officials, an inmate's medical care level can change over time because he or she can develop chronic care conditions during imprisonment.

[24]The conference report, H.R. Conf. Rep. No. 107-278, at 83 (2001), accompanying the Departments of Commerce, Justice, and State, the Judiciary, and Related Agencies Appropriations Act, 2002, Pub. L. No. 107-77, 115 Stat. 748 (Nov. 28, 2001), stated that "[t]he conference agreement provides that of the $650,047,000 provided for increases as outlined below, $5,000,000 shall be for partial site and planning of the USP Northeast/Mid-Atlantic facility, to be located in Berlin, New Hampshire."

[25]The conference report, H.R. Con. Rep. No. 106-1005, at 220 (2000), accompanying the District of Columbia Appropriations Act, 2001, Pub. L. No. 106-553, 114 Stat. 2762 (Dec. 21, 2000), stated that "[t]he conference agreement adopts the Senate report language directing BOP to continue to assess the feasibility of construction of a high-security facility in Yazoo City, MS, as described in the Senate report."

environmental impact statements.[26] In contrast, BOP's annual congressional budget justification is used to convey BOP's funding and housing needs, and these justifications would allow DOJ and BOP officials the opportunity to convey to Congress any potential challenges BOP may be facing or anticipating with respect to selecting certain sites for new institutions.

According to BOP officials, when BOP is congressionally directed to investigate a particular location, BOP generally considers this as a direction to focus its efforts on constructing an institution in that specific location. However, officials from both BOP's Central Office and activating institutions acknowledged that the locations of these newly constructed institutions make activation more difficult. *Standards for Internal Control in the Federal Government* states that management should ensure that there are adequate means of communicating with, and obtaining information from, external stakeholders, such as Congress, that may have a significant impact on the agency achieving its goals.[27] Since delayed activations limit BOP's ability to reduce crowding as BOP intended, DOJ and BOP would be better positioned for future activations and could more effectively manage activation costs and timelines by using BOP's annual congressional budget justification to communicate to Congress the factors that might delay future activations, such as challenges hiring staff and placing inmates, associated with the locations of new institutions. In turn, congressional decision makers could be better positioned to take such factors into account when directing BOP where to build new institutions.

---

[26]Environmental assessments describe how an institution would affect the physical environment, such as air quality, and the socioeconomics of the local area, such as the unemployment rate. Environmental impact statements are more detailed than environmental assessments.

[27]GAO, *Standards for Internal Control in the Federal Government*, GAO/AIMD-00-21.3.1 (Washington, D.C.: Nov. 1999). Further, we recommended in December 2013 that BOP could better ensure that it meets congressional stakeholders' needs by consulting with congressional decision makers to determine if it would be helpful to include additional funding details in its annual budget justification. GAO, *Bureau of Prisons: Opportunities Exist to Enhance the Transparency of Annual Budget Justifications,* GAO-14-121 (Washington, D.C.: Dec. 6, 2013). DOJ agreed with our recommendation.

BOP Does Not Analyze Staffing Data at the Institution Level to Mitigate Staffing Challenges

BOP's Central Office reviews aggregated data of staffing system-wide, but it does not monitor or analyze staffing data by individual institutions, such as those located on a complex, or track how long it takes individual activating institutions to hire staff. When we analyzed OPM's EHRI data on BOP staffing, we found that none of the institutions in the activation process has a full complement of staff.[28] Although the following institutions are partially activated, FCI Aliceville is 63 percent staffed, FCI Berlin is 67 percent staffed, and FCI Mendota is 73 percent staffed.[29] Since these institutions are not fully staffed, they cannot be fully activated until they have a full complement of staff to effectively manage additional inmates.

Standards for Internal Control in the Federal Government calls for agencies to identify, capture, and distribute operational data to determine whether an agency is meeting its goals and effectively using resources.[30] Because BOP's Central Office does not review staffing data at the institution level, BOP's human resources officials from the Central Office could not tell us whether all of the specific institutions in our review, specifically those located on complexes, faced obstacles recruiting and retaining staff. Likewise, BOP officials were not positioned to discuss the impact of potential staffing challenges on activation. Such staffing challenges could affect how quickly BOP can reduce crowding across the system—one of BOP's key strategic goals.

According to BOP officials, they could analyze available data by institution by reallocating staff to conduct such an analysis. However, BOP has not made such monitoring a priority because, as BOP officials told us, wardens of institutions are ultimately responsible for ensuring that institutions are properly staffed. In addition, our analysis demonstrates that each institution has experienced recruiting and retention challenges. For example, although two of the three partially activated institutions have experienced increases in the number of staff it hires each fiscal year,

---

[28]OPM's EHRI database is the primary government-wide source for information on federal employees. EHRI contains information on personnel actions and other data for most federal civilian employees. These data are as of September 30, 2013.

[29]OPM's EHRI data are reported by complex, rather than by institution. As a result, we were unable to use these data to accurately determine the extent to which FCI Hazelton and USP Yazoo City were staffed since they are both located on complexes.

[30]GAO/AIMD-00-21.3.1.

where institutions hired staff at higher rates in each consecutive year, authorized positions remained unfilled. In addition, for example, not all of the employees FCI Mendota hired from fiscal years 2010 through 2013 remained on board to work at the institution. Additionally, our analysis of OPM data indicates that each institution undergoing activation has had staff sever employment with BOP or transfer to other institutions, compounding existing staffing issues. For instance, each year more staff have separated from employment at FCI Mendota than in the prior year, for a total of 40 employees—about 21 percent of its total hires—from fiscal years 2010 through 2013.[31] Additionally, according to data provided by BOP from its personnel database for fiscal year 2014—through July—an additional 11 employees separated from FCI Mendota. See appendix II for our analysis of BOP's human resources data.

BOP currently provides some relocation benefits and salaries above the minimum rate to any institution struggling to hire sufficient staff, including those undergoing activation.[32] However, these incentives have not effectively addressed the challenges that activating institutions face hiring staff. Specifically, BOP officials said that BOP has the authority to offer incentives in order to recruit and retain qualified staff for positions that are difficult to fill, either because they are specialty positions, such as medical personnel, or because they are located at institutions in remote locations.[33] According to BOP data, BOP offered incentives a total of 150 times for a combined total of about $1.1 million as a means of recruiting potential new hires to the institutions in our review, and 147 of those incentives were ultimately accepted by new hires.[34] Although BOP Central Office officials stated that these incentives were used frequently, the staffing challenges continue to delay activation. Without analyzing staffing data, such as recruiting and retention data, at individual activating institutions, BOP is not positioned to assess its progress toward reaching

---

[31]During this time frame, there were likely also existing BOP staff that transferred in and out of that institution.

[32]OPM defines the minimum rate as the minimum wage an employee may be paid based on the employee's scheduled rate of pay.

[33]BOP cited three legal authorities allowing it to use incentives for attracting candidates in hard-to-fill positions: 5 C.F.R. § 575.106 (recruitment incentives), 5 C.F.R. § 575.206 (relocation incentives), and 5 C.F.R. § 575.306 (retention incentives).

[34]According to BOP, more than 1 incentive could be offered to a potential applicant.

authorized staffing levels or to develop effective, tailored strategies to mitigate those challenges.

BOP Does Not Have a Policy to Guide Activation or a Schedule That Meets Best Practices

BOP institutions in the activation process rely on the expertise of staff and two templates that the Central Office developed to guide the activation process: (1) the activation handbook, which identifies roles and responsibilities for BOP officials during the activation process, and (2) the staffing timeline, which provides a general sequence of hiring events that BOP staff are to follow prior to the institution receiving inmates. Activating institutions complete these templates, and may modify the documents at their discretion; thus, they differ in style, scope, and substance depending on the institution completing them. However, the two templates do not constitute a documented, bureau-wide policy related to activation, nor do they include an activation schedule that incorporates best practices, such as accounting for factors that might delay activation, including delays in receiving congressionally directed activation funding or challenges with staffing institutions.

No Documented Activation Policy

Activating institutions in our review did not have a detailed policy or schedule to guide the activation process. Instead, they relied heavily on relationships with individuals who had experience with activations. For example, officials at half of the institutions told us that they relied on the experience of officials who had previously been involved with activations to help guide the process. Further, on our site visit to USP Yazoo City, officials told us that the primary challenge related to financial management during the activation process was ensuring that the managers of each of the departments in the institution, such as business administration or human resources, knew what was required for activation. The business administrator sought out assistance from the regional office and visited another institution that was activated prior to USP Yazoo City to review records and itemized lists of what officials had determined they needed for that activation. Further, BOP relied on the experience of a now-retired official serving as the Activation Coordinator for the institutions in our review. BOP relied on that official to initiate the activation process by ordering necessary supplies and equipment. Officials we interviewed from the regional offices noted that without the Activation Coordinator's guidance, they would not have known what supplies and equipment were needed for activation. *Standards for Internal Control in the Federal Government* states that policies and procedures are needed to enforce management's directives, and that significant events need to be documented in policies and procedures.[35] According to BOP documents and officials, BOP does not plan to construct, and subsequently activate, new institutions for the foreseeable future. In addition, officials contend that BOP has vast institutional knowledge to guide the activation process, rendering a formal written policy unnecessary. Nevertheless, BOP will likely face difficulty during future activations since about 32 percent of BOP staff will be retirement eligible within 5 fiscal years—a proportion that is similar to the retirement rate for the federal workforce as a whole. Such staffing attrition underscores the need to have documented policies in place to ensure that future staff can conduct and complete activations effectively and within cost and schedule commitments.

Activation Schedule Does Not Meet Best Practices

According to our analysis of the details included in each institution's version of the activation handbook template and the staffing timeline template, we determined that BOP's schedules do not meet all 10 best practices required for a schedule to be reliable. Specifically, we assessed each of the six institutions' versions of the activation handbook and staffing timeline templates against four characteristics of a reliable schedule associated with the 10 best practices.[36] As table 1 shows, collectively, the six BOP institutions minimally met two and did not meet two of these four characteristics.

Table 1: Extent to Which the Federal Bureau of Prisons' (BOP) Schedules Met Best Practices

Characteristic	Characteristic description	Assessment
Comprehensive	A schedule should reflect all activities.	Minimally met
Controlled	A schedule should be continuously updated using logic, durations, and actual progress to realistically forecast dates for program activities.	Minimally met
Well constructed	A schedule should be planned so that critical project dates can be met.	Not met
Credible	A schedule should include data on risks and opportunities for the project, and a level of confidence in meeting a project's completion date based on those data.	Not met

Source: GAO analysis of BOP schedule documentation. I GAO-14-709

---

[35]GAO/AIMD-00-21.3.1.

[36]GAO-12-120G.

The activation handbook template and general staffing timeline template that BOP's Central Office provides are positive steps toward a schedule that could be used to guide future institution activations because they provide some level of detail regarding the activities required for activation. However, as illustrated in table 1, collectively, institutions' versions of the activation handbook and the staffing timeline templates minimally met the criteria for being comprehensive or controlled and did not meet the criteria for being well constructed or credible, which are aspects of reliable schedules.

Comprehensive. We reviewed the activation handbook and staffing timeline templates that each of the six institutions completed and found that they minimally met the requirements for a comprehensive schedule. The activation handbook template contains some elements key to having a comprehensive schedule, such as listing necessary tasks, organized by responsible departments or contractors. However, the activation handbook template provides the tasks, or activities, in the list in a general way, but none of the six institutions tailored the tasks to meet their specific requirements, limiting the bureau's ability to oversee all activation activities. Similarly, the activation handbook template does not fully include details on all of the necessary resources to do the work associated with each activity and does not identify the specific personnel within the department responsible for each activity. Finally, none of the six institutions included any reference to project duration in its respective activation handbook. Without information about the estimated length of time required to complete each activity, management cannot accurately identify the staffing resources required to complete it, assess the progress of the activation process, or establish realistic dates for institution activation. With respect to the general staffing timeline template that BOP's Central Office provides, this document roughly identifies when particular staff resources are needed based on the anticipated activation date. However, the general staffing timeline template is based on the anticipated activation date rather than based on the activities each of the staff would be doing—and none of the six institutions made modifications to elaborate on these activities. Because of these deficiencies, the information contained in each of the six institutions' activation handbooks and staffing timelines does not assist management in forecasting whether activities will be completed as scheduled or as budgeted. Further, these documents do not allow insight into the allocation of resources, increasing the likelihood that the activation process will not be completed as anticipated and limiting BOP's ability to ensure accountability for the total scope of work.

Controlled. The activation handbook and staffing timeline templates that each of the six institutions modified minimally met the requirements for a controlled schedule. Two of the activating institutions provided versions of BOP's activation handbook and staffing timeline templates that contained some indication that information on key dates and activities was updated at some point in time by the activating institutions. However, the activation handbook and staffing timeline templates modified by each institution did not indicate whether they had been updated at regular intervals, or that they reflected the actual status of the respective activations. Further, none of the activating institutions' activation handbooks or staffing timelines included the status of key milestone dates, such as whether specific activities had been completed, or when the activation should be completed. In addition, none of the activating institutions used the activation handbook and staffing timelines to describe the critical risks that the institution faced in meeting its goals for activation or contingencies if those risks were realized, such as challenges with staffing. Without regularly updating the schedule based on the current status of the activation at each respective institution, BOP is limited in its ability to monitor activation progress or make decisions on how to mitigate risk or allocate resources for activating institutions.

Well Constructed. The activation handbook and staffing timeline templates that each of the six institutions modified did not meet the requirements for a well-constructed schedule, because the activation handbook and staffing timeline documents did not provide specific information regarding start and finish dates, durations, or sequencing of activation-related activities. As a result, BOP does not have insight about the interdependencies between activities or the way in which early delays in some activities could affect activities later on as well as the overall activation completion date. Additionally, without identifying linkages between activities, BOP does not know the critical path of the activation process—that is, which activities can and cannot be delayed if the overall schedule is to be met. This prevents the agency from providing Congress with reliable timeline estimates or anticipated activation dates.

Credible. The activation handbook and staffing timeline templates that each of the six institutions modified did not meet the requirements for a credible schedule. A credible schedule is horizontally integrated, where products and outcomes are linked with other associated sequenced activities, which helps verify that activities are arranged in the right order to achieve aggregated products or outcomes. A credible schedule is also vertically integrated to ensure that the start and completion dates for activities are aligned with such dates on subsidiary schedules supporting tasks and subtasks. With respect to the best practice of vertically and horizontally aligning activities, two institutions adapted BOP's activation handbook template to insert targeted due dates for selected activities, but neither identified subset activities or linked overall activities in any specific order to achieve full horizontal or vertical integration. Without such integration, BOP is not positioned to ensure that subactivities are on track for an overall activity's completion.

The activation handbook and staffing timeline templates that BOP developed and that are modified by activating institutions are positive steps toward a baseline schedule that could be used to guide future institution activations, because they provide some level of detail regarding the activities required for activation. However, the activation handbook and staffing timeline templates contain only limited information consistent with best practices and therefore cannot be used by management to reliably measure, monitor, or report on performance. Appendix III contains our detailed assessment for each characteristic and the reasons BOP minimally met or did not meet the best practices.

BOP officials stated that each institution undergoing activation generally follows the same process and is guided by experienced officials at both the Central Office and the regional offices, which, in the past, included the experience of an Activation Coordinator. In particular, according to BOP officials, activation of new institutions follows standardized processes that allow BOP to generally predict accurate timelines for activation. However, as discussed above, each of the activating institutions is behind schedule, which indicates that the schedules used during activation may not adequately ensure that activation occurs within schedule estimates. BOP officials acknowledged that scheduling delays can occur, and when they do, it is usually because of delays in congressionally directed funding or difficulty with hiring. BOP officials stated that, generally, BOP does not start the activation process until it has received congressionally directed activation funding, and because of this, according to DOJ officials, activation schedules are inherently affected by the availability and timing of the agency's final funding level for a fiscal year. Because BOP officials consider that the activation clock does not start until it receives such funding, they do not consider it an activation process delay on their part if a delay in receiving such funding causes an institution to be activated later than was originally planned. However, our analysis showed that the activation handbook and staffing timeline documents used as schedules by the six institutions did not contain contingencies related to external factors, such as receiving congressionally directed activation funding. A comprehensive policy with a schedule that is well constructed and credible, for example, could be used to reflect how delays in receiving congressionally directed activation funding might affect activating institutions within schedule estimates and improve the quality of information that BOP provides to Congress regarding the status of the activation process.

Because the activation handbook does not fully reflect a standardized list of all of the activities required for activation, management cannot ensure that the total scope of work is accounted for by the handbook. Consequently, BOP is limited in its ability to minimize the potential for delays in the activation process. Developing and implementing a comprehensive activation policy that incorporates the knowledge of staff with experience activating institutions could help equip BOP staff with the expertise and resources needed to efficiently activate new institutions. Additionally, having a schedule that incorporates the four characteristics of scheduling best practices could better position BOP staff to activate institutions in accordance with realistic schedule commitments and to navigate potential obstacles that may arise, thereby saving the bureau time and resources.

BOP Obligated Funds from Two Accounts to Maintain Partially Activated Institutions

From fiscal year 2010 through March 2014, BOP obligated about $25 million from its S&E account to maintain partially activated institutions while it waited for congressionally directed activation funding through the S&E account. The amount of congressionally directed activation funding included in BOP's annual spend plans reflects the amount the bureau planned to spend activating each of the individual institutions in our review from fiscal year 2010 through March 2014.[37] However, we found that BOP obligated more than its planned amount for two of the three partially activated institutions (see table 2).

[37]After an agency or component receives an appropriation, agencies develop plans for how they will spend that funding. We reviewed BOP's spend plans from fiscal years 2010 through 2014—the fiscal years for which BOP received congressionally directed funding for activation.

Table 2: Federal Bureau of Prisons' (BOP) Congressionally Directed Activation Funding and Actual Obligations from Its Salaries and Expenses (S&E) Account for Partially Activated Institutions from Fiscal Year 2010 through March 2014

Institution	Total congressionally directed activation funding from BOP's S&E account	Total actual obligations from BOP's S&E account[a]	Amount obligated from BOP's S&E account while waiting for activation funding[b]
FCI Aliceville	$51,457,000	$47,391,800	0
FCI Berlin	50,195,000	57,713,200	7,518,200
FCI Mendota	49,400,000	67,077,300	17,677,300
Total	**$151,052,000**	**$172,182,300**	**$25,195,500**

Source: GAO analysis of BOP data. I GAO-14-709

Note: We included institutions in this analysis only for which BOP is no longer obligating activation funds. According to BOP officials, it has not finished obligating funding for activities related to the activation of Federal Correctional Institution (FCI) Hazelton, U.S. Penitentiary (USP) Yazoo City, or Administrative USP Thomson. Accordingly, the extent to which BOP will spend what it planned on activating those institutions is not yet clear.

[a]These obligations represent the cumulative obligations made from fiscal year 2010 through March 2014.

[b]BOP receives congressionally directed activation funding through its S&E account. When such congressionally directed activation funding has been delayed, BOP has obligated funding from the S&E account, which is generally used to fund the operation of all BOP institutions, to maintain partially activated institutions. For FCI Berlin and FCI Mendota, this amount represents the difference between the amount BOP planned to spend and what it actually obligated. Because BOP obligated less than it planned for FCI Aliceville, BOP did not obligate any funds from its S&E account while waiting for congressionally directed activation funding for that institution.

Specifically, BOP obligated about $7.5 million and $17.7 million more than it planned to activate FCI Berlin and FCI Mendota, respectively, for a collective total of about $25.2 million more than it estimated in its spend plan. Additionally, we found that BOP's obligations for activating those three institutions are similar to what BOP has spent in the past when activating new institutions. Specifically, when adjusting for inflation, BOP spent, on average, about $41,100 per bed for those institutions, and spent, on average, about $40,600 per bed on the 21 institutions activated from 1994 through 2000.[38]

---

[38]We adjusted for inflation all obligations made for partially activated institutions and divided those by the total number of beds that these institutions and their respective camps provide for each fiscal year from 2010 through 2014. Without adjusting for inflation, BOP spent, on average, about $39,600 per bed on partially activated institutions in our review, and, on average, $29,200 per bed on the 21 institutions constructed from 1994 through 2000.

To finance the additional $25 million of activation-related activities, BOP officials told us they used S&E funds that are generally used to fund the operation of all BOP institutions. Specifically, BOP officials told us that BOP spends between $1 million and $4 million each year to maintain a newly constructed or acquired institution while waiting for the congressionally directed activation funding needed to complete the activation process. This additional spending supports, among other things, salaries of a core group of staff and the cost of utilities to maintain institutions and keep them secure prior to receiving congressionally directed activation funding. According to BOP officials, when BOP is waiting for congressionally directed activation funding for a given institution, BOP hires a facility manager to ensure that the building is operating appropriately and covers costs associated with utilities, such as electricity and water. For example, to maintain Administrative USP Thomson while waiting for congressionally directed activation funding, BOP obligated $1.3 million in fiscal year 2013, and, as of March 2014, BOP has obligated about $440,700. Those costs included relocation expenses, uniforms, and training for the maintenance staff; utilities; and mechanical services for the institution, among other things. In addition, BOP officials told us that BOP spent about $150,000 over 2 fiscal years to fund a state of Illinois employee to maintain the institution while waiting for BOP staff to be hired. Further, BOP spent about $10 million in utility and personnel costs to maintain FCI Berlin for an additional 2 fiscal years while BOP waited for congressionally directed activation funding to begin activation. According to BOP officials, that additional funding covered the salary expenses for 16 employees that the agency hired to maintain the institution. BOP officials told us they had planned on paying for these salaries with its requested activation funding, but because the activation funding was delayed, BOP used other available funds from its S&E account to keep the staff in place.

In addition to maintaining empty institutions while waiting for congressionally directed activation funding, BOP has also obligated funds from its B&F account to provide a range of modifications to new institutions after construction is complete. According to BOP data, BOP spent a total of about $1.2 million on alterations, installations, and repairs at four of the six institutions in our review, with costs per institution ranging from about $130,000 to $458,000. For example, FCI Berlin spent $150,000 repairing roofs that could not handle the heavy amounts of snowfall and constructing overhangs at exterior doorways to provide protection from the weather.[39] BOP officials told us that additional costs are generally related to maintaining empty institutions because of a lag in receiving activation funds. As discussed earlier in this report, communicating the potential challenges that certain locations may pose for activation could help BOP minimize the amount of renovation or staff relocation expenses it ultimately spends while awaiting congressionally directed activation funding.

The Six Institutions Being Activated Will Reduce Crowding System-wide when They Reach Rated Capacity

BOP plans to activate and fully populate all six institutions with inmates by fiscal year 2016, which would add 7,852 beds to BOP's overall capacity.[40] If BOP achieves this goal, these institutions will reduce the overall crowding rate from almost 42 percent to 34 percent. According to our estimates using BOP's projections of the future inmate population, we found that crowding reductions will vary for inmates depending on their gender and security level. To determine how these institutions will affect system-wide crowding, we compared crowding rates with and without the addition of new beds that BOP anticipates the six institutions will provide by fiscal year 2016. On the basis of that comparison, we estimate that BOP will have spent almost $200 million per percentage point decrease in the overall crowding rate—or about $1.6 billion since fiscal year 2003—on constructing, acquiring, and activating the institutions in our review. For specific details on these institutions' impact on crowding, see table 3.

---

[39]Officials explained that the construction contractor contended that the building's flat roof, which is part of BOP's standard design, was not appropriate for the heavy snowfall in northern New Hampshire and took steps to limit its liability for weather-related warranty repairs. BOP's Design and Construction Branch staff explained that they routinely review and modify designs as necessary, but told us the construction contractor determines how the roof of an institution will be built, and the material of the roof determines whether or not the roofs are pitched or flat.

[40]This number includes the additional beds provided by the individual institutions in our review only. This number does not include the beds provided by each institution's respective minimum-security camp, because camps were outside the scope of our review.

Table 3: Anticipated Federal Bureau of Prisons' (BOP) Before-and-After Crowding Rates, Assuming Institutions Reach Rated Capacity in Fiscal Year 2016 and Associated Obligations Data

	Crowding rate in fiscal year 2016 if institutions in our review do not house any inmates (before)[a]	Crowding rate in fiscal year 2016 if institutions in our review are fully populated (after)	Anticipated percentage point reduction in crowding	Total obligations made to construct and activate institutions in our review[b]	Obligations made per percentage point decrease in crowding rate
Overall	42%	34%	-8%	$1,582,575,403	$204,231,529
By gender					
Overall male	41	34	-7	1,309,691,973	175,247,023
Overall female	45	24	-21	272,883,430	12,761,393
Security level					
Medium male	55	42	-13	918,947,210	72,087,213
High male	57	31	-26	390,744,763	14,945,386
Low female	84	28	-56	272,883,430	4,890,524

Source: GAO analysis of BOP data. I GAO-14-709

[a]The estimated crowding rates are based on BOP's estimates of the future inmate population in fiscal year 2016. Fiscal year 2016 is the year when BOP anticipates that each of the institutions in our review will be fully activated.

[b]We totaled BOP data on obligations BOP made to construct or acquire and activate Federal Correctional Institution (FCI) Aliceville, FCI Berlin, FCI Hazelton, FCI Mendota, U.S. Penitentiary (USP) Yazoo City, and Administrative USP Thomson. To calculate the obligations made by security level, we totaled obligations for institutions with corresponding gender and security levels.

Crowding by gender. The new institutions housing male inmates will add a total of 6,316 beds to total capacity once they are fully activated. The addition of these beds will reduce crowding among male institutions by about 7 percentage points, lowering the rate from about 41 percent to about 34 percent, assuming that the institutions will reach rated capacity by fiscal year 2016 as BOP intends. Similarly, the only new institution to add beds for female institutions, FCI Aliceville, will add a total of 1,536 beds to total capacity for institutions housing female inmates. The addition of these beds will reduce crowding among female institutions by about 21 percentage points, falling from about 45 percent to about 24 percent.

Crowding by security level. The new institutions housing medium-security inmates will add a total of 3,456 beds, while the new institutions housing high-security inmates will add a total of 2,860 beds, once they are fully activated. Additionally, the new institution housing low-security female inmates will add 1,536 inmates. The addition of medium-security beds at FCI Berlin, FCI Hazelton, and FCI Mendota will reduce crowding at that security level by about 13 percentage points, lowering the crowding rate from about 55 percent to about 42 percent, assuming that the new institutions will reach rated capacity by fiscal year 2016 as BOP intends. Similarly, the addition of high-security beds at Administrative USP Thomson and USP Yazoo City will reduce crowding at that security level by about 26 percent, lowering the crowding rate from about 57 percent to 31 percent. Finally, once fully activated, FCI Aliceville will reduce crowding among low-security female institutions by about 56 percentage points, or a decrease from about 84 percent to about 28 percent. Because FCI Aliceville will add 1,536 beds to an overall capacity of 5,048 beds among medium-security institutions housing female inmates, these new beds will have a large effect on crowding at that security level.

DOJ Purchased Thomson to Reduce High-Security Crowding, but It Will Increase Costs

DOJ purchased the Thomson Correctional Center in an effort to reduce high-security crowding, and if the institution reaches rated capacity by fiscal year 2016, we estimate that the institution will reduce high-security crowding by about 16 percentage points. However, purchasing Thomson resulted in unplanned costs at the time of the purchase and will increase costs in the future.

DOJ Purchased Thomson to Provide High-Security Bed Space and Used Several Accounts to Finance the Purchase

DOJ stated in its budget requests that acquiring the Thomson Correctional Center in Illinois would address high-security crowding and support BOP's mission, as well as DOJ's strategic goal to ensure the fair and efficient administration of justice. The state of Illinois constructed the institution in 2001 to address inmate crowding in state-operated institutions, but never populated the high-security portion of the institution with inmates because of the institution's high operating costs, among other things. In December 2009, the President issued a memorandum to the Attorney General and Secretary of Defense directing DOJ and the Department of Defense to purchase and use the Thomson Correctional Center.[41] The memorandum stated that the acquisition of the institution would facilitate the closure of detention facilities at Guantanamo Bay

---

[41]The President, *Memorandum of December 15, 2009—Directing Certain Actions with Respect to Acquisition and Use of Thomson Correctional Center to Facilitate Closure of Detention Facilities in Guantanamo Naval Base,* Federal Register Vol. 74, No. 241 (Washington, D.C.: Dec. 15, 2009).

Naval Base and reduce BOP's shortage of high-security, maximum-custody bed space. However, legislation limited or prohibited the use of federal funds to transfer Guantanamo Bay detainees into the United States,[42] and DOJ officials stated that the department was committed to fully adhering to those prohibitions. DOJ pursued the purchase of the institution to provide beds for high-security inmates who, according to DOJ officials, were not previously detained at Guantanamo Bay.

DOJ requested funding from Congress to purchase and activate the Thomson Correctional Center in its annual budget requests for fiscal years 2011 and 2012. Congress did not provide funding for either request. While DOJ continued to wait for specific funding for the acquisition of the Thomson Correctional Center, DOJ and the state of Illinois assessed the purchase of the institution. During this time, DOJ obtained two appraisals indicating an average value of $165 million, and the state of Illinois conducted three appraisals. On the basis of the average value from the two appraisals conducted on behalf of the federal government, DOJ and the state of Illinois agreed on a price of $165 million (the compensation for the taking of the property by the federal government as described below).[43]

Congress did not provide specific funding to finance the purchase of the Thomson Correctional Center. Therefore, in July 2012, DOJ notified the Senate and House Committees on Appropriations of its intention to allocate $165 million in existing funding to purchase the institution.[44] DOJ

---

[42]See Supplemental Appropriations Act, 2009, Pub. L. No. 111-32, 123 Stat. 1859 (June 24, 2009). Congress continued to pass legislation limiting or prohibiting the use of federal funds to transfer Guantanamo Bay detainees to U.S. facilities. See, e.g., National Defense Authorization Act for Fiscal Year 2010, Pub. L. No. 111-84, 123 Stat. 2190 (Oct. 28, 2009); Consolidated Appropriations Act, 2010, Pub. L. No. 111-117, 123 Stat. 3034 (Dec. 16, 2009); Ike Skelton National Defense Authorization Act for Fiscal Year 2011, Pub. L. No. 111-383, 123 Stat. 4137 (Jan. 7, 2011); and National Defense Authorization Act for Fiscal Year 2012, Pub. L. No. 112-81, 125 Stat. 1298 (Dec. 31, 2011).

[43]Additionally, BOP estimates that it will cost $25 million to renovate Administrative USP Thomson for a total acquisition and renovation cost of $190 million. Further, in its fiscal year 2014 spend plan, BOP included $43.7 million to begin activation of USP Thomson.

[44]DOJ provided a notification letter to the appropriations committees in response to requirements of the Consolidated and Further Continuing Appropriations Act, 2012, as it related to the reprogramming and transferring of appropriated funds in BOP's annual appropriation, as well as 28 U.S.C. § 524(c)(8)(E), as it related to the transferring of funds from the Assets Forfeiture Fund Super Surplus.

and BOP allocated funds from three separate funding sources. Specifically, BOP reprogrammed $5 million in its B&F appropriation from the modernization and repair subaccount into the B&F new construction subaccount,[45] and transferred $9 million from BOP's S&E account to BOP's B&F account.[46] In addition, DOJ transferred $151 million from DOJ's Assets Forfeiture Fund Super Surplus to BOP's B&F account.[47] According to DOJ and BOP budget officials, the absence of specific funding for purchasing the Thomson Correctional Center, and restrictions on transferring and reprogramming applicable to BOP's annual appropriations affected DOJ's decisions to use these multiple funding streams.[48] In September 2012, the Director of BOP filed in the United States District Court for the Northern District of Illinois a "declaration of taking" to acquire the Thomson Correctional Center and deposited the $165 million with the court as compensation. In October 2012, DOJ

---

[45]Reprogramming is a shifting of funds from one purpose to another within a single appropriation.

[46]A transfer is the shifting of funds between appropriations.

[47]Every year, federal, state, and local law enforcement agencies seize millions of dollars in assets that are forfeited through the DOJ Assets Forfeiture Program. Forfeited assets can include, but are not limited to, businesses, cash, bank accounts, automobiles, boats, airplanes, jewelry, art objects, and real estate. Under the statutory authority of 28 U.S.C. § 524(c)(8)(E), subject to certain notification procedures, any excess unobligated balance remaining in the Assets Forfeiture Fund Super Surplus is available to the Attorney General for any federal law enforcement, litigative/prosecutive, and correctional activities, or any other authorized purpose of DOJ. Further, any amounts provided could be used under the authorities available to the organization receiving the funds.

[48]Section 205 of the Consolidated and Further Continuing Appropriations Act, 2012, provided that "not to exceed 5 percent of *any appropriation made available for the current fiscal year for the Department of Justice in this Act* may be transferred between such appropriations, (emphasis added)" which limited the amount BOP could transfer from its S&E account. Additionally, the Act provided that "*no such appropriation*, except as otherwise specifically provided, shall be increased by more than 10 percent *by any such transfers*, (emphasis added)" which limited the amount that the B&F account could accept from any appropriation made available for fiscal year 2012 for DOJ in the Act. Pub. L. No. 112-55, § 205, 125 Stat. 552, 619. Section 205 of the Act provided that any transfer conducted pursuant to the section was to be treated as a reprogramming of funds under section 505 of the Act. Under section 505 of the Act, none of the funds provided under the Act would be available for obligation or expenditure through certain types of reprogramming of funds unless the House and Senate Committees on Appropriations were notified 15 days in advance of such reprogramming of funds. Pub. L. No. 112-55, § 505, 125 Stat. 552, 630-31.

acquired the Thomson Correctional Center from the state of Illinois and subsequently renamed the institution Administrative USP Thomson.[49]

Purchasing Thomson Will Address Crowding at the High-Security Level, but Will Result in Increased Operational Costs

Once it reaches rated capacity, according to our analysis of inmate population data, Administrative USP Thomson will help address crowding at the high-security level by about 16 percent for male inmates, which is similar to the decrease in crowding rates that DOJ asserted in the business cases submitted to Congress as part of the annual budget process. The expenses associated with the initial purchase price shifted funds away from BOP repairs and program services, and the continued expenses of operating and maintaining the institution will incur future costs. BOP officials acknowledged that the purchase of Administrative USP Thomson posed costs at the time of the purchase and will pose costs in the future, but said that the benefits that Administrative USP Thomson provides—particularly high-security bed space—far outweigh the costs associated with the institution. The activation of any new institution, including Administrative USP Thomson, will increase BOP's operational costs. Further, according to DOJ officials, the purchase of Administrative USP Thomson provided bed space at a lower cost than constructing a new institution.

The $14 million DOJ used from BOP's S&E and B&F accounts toward the purchase of Administrative USP Thomson came from accounts that BOP uses for the operation and maintenance of the federal prison system. Specifically, BOP uses funds from the B&F account's modernization and repair subaccount to address outstanding, unfunded modernization and repair items system-wide, otherwise known as BOP's maintenance and repair backlog. BOP maintains a list of these backlogged items that are in excess of $300,000, such as replacing roofs and boilers, that it considers important in order to rehabilitate, modernize, and otherwise repair physical structures and systems needed to maintain safety and security at its institutions and avoid costlier repairs in the future. BOP's list from 2012 totaled approximately $346 million and included 150 items, the most

---

[49]DOJ acquired the Thomson Correctional Center through eminent domain, a process by which the federal government can obtain property from other entities. Pursuant to 40 U.S.C. § 3113, "[a]n officer of the Federal Government authorized to acquire real estate for the erection of a public building or for other public uses may acquire the real estate for the Government by condemnation, under judicial process, when the officer believes it is necessary or advantageous to the Government to do so."

expensive of which was about $16 million. Since Thomson is a 13-year-old facility and will incur repair costs as it ages, it may add new items to BOP's existing list of unfunded maintenance and repair priorities. BOP's S&E account funds staffing, inmate medical care, food, utilities, and services at various BOP institutions, such as inmate educational or vocational programs, among other things. In addition, during the nearly 2 years BOP has owned Administrative USP Thomson, it has spent approximately $1.8 million from the S&E account to maintain the empty facility while waiting for activation funding.

BOP estimates that once Administrative USP Thomson is fully activated, it will cost $160 million each year to operate it as a high-security institution that primarily houses special management unit (SMU) inmates.[50] Of that amount, $45 million is expected to cover food, medical, clothing, laundry, utilities, programming, and other related operating expenses, and $115 million is expected to cover staff salary and benefit costs. This $160 million estimated total annual operating cost is higher than that for all but two other BOP institutions, Federal Correctional Complex (FCC) Butner and FCC Coleman, based on fiscal year 2013 operational cost data.[51] In BOP's fiscal year 2014 congressional budget request, BOP estimated the need for 1,158 correctional positions at Administrative USP Thomson, 749 of which will be positions for correctional officers.[52] SMUs require more staff than institutions with lower security levels because more staff are needed to provide constant inmate supervision. BOP officials told us that Administrative USP Thomson will require a large number of staff to operate because BOP plans to move some of the most dangerous SMU inmates housed elsewhere into Administrative USP Thomson.

---

[50]SMU inmates are housed in a type of segregated housing unit used to separate inmates from the general population for different purposes—such as disciplinary reasons, gang-related activity, or assaulting staff. SMU inmates are part of a four-level program where they progress from more restrictive to less constrictive conditions.

[51]FCC Butner is a large complex consisting of four separate institutions and a camp, and its staff provide medical services to inmates requiring an advanced level of care. FCC Coleman is also a large complex consisting of four separate institutions (two at the high-security level) and a camp, and it has the largest number of inmates of any BOP facility.

[52]BOP officials told us that the remaining correctional positions will be for staff necessary for operating the institution.

Administrative USP Thomson has a rated capacity of 2,100 beds—1,900 high-security SMU beds and 200 minimum-security beds at the onsite camp—and, according to BOP officials, the potential to use some of its high-security rated capacity to house up to 400 ADX inmates. Additionally, BOP officials told us that they estimate the institution eventually will be overcrowded by about 30 percent, given current and projected inmate population levels system-wide. Accordingly, they estimate that Administrative USP Thomson will ultimately house between 2,600 and 3,000 inmates. While this level of crowding would be lower than the current rate of 52 percent at BOP's other high-security institutions, the daily cost per inmate at Administrative USP Thomson will still exceed the daily cost per inmate for SMU bed space at USP Lewisburg, which is the only other institution whose USP entirely houses SMU inmates.[53] Specifically, we estimate that BOP will spend between $146.12 and $168.60 each day per inmate housed at Administrative USP Thomson and its camp. In comparison, we estimate that BOP spends about $100.46 daily per inmate for all inmates at USP Lewisburg (i.e., the SMU and camp inmates). This cost rises to $123.33 daily for only those inmates in its SMU.[54]

BOP included funding to activate Administrative USP Thomson in its fiscal year 2014 spend plan and anticipates that it will be fully activated by fiscal year 2016. As of July 2014, BOP had not determined how many inmates the institution will house, including how many ADX beds will be necessary. As we found in 2013, BOP has had empty ADX beds in Florence since fiscal year 2008. We also found that, according to BOP officials, the ADX population has declined overall because, among other things, BOP has placed inmates in SMUs instead of in the ADX institution.[55] Given that BOP expects to begin activation at Administrative USP Thomson this fiscal year, and is behind its target date for completing

---

[53]USP Lewisburg also has a minimum security camp onsite.

[54]We divided BOP's estimate by the number of inmates it estimates that the institution will house—2,600 inmates in one case and 3,000 inmates in another case— to provide the range in annual costs per inmate. We then divided the annual costs by 365 days in the calendar year to arrive at daily cost per inmate. BOP's daily cost per inmate varies depending on the number of inmates housed at the institution. BOP previously provided daily inmate costs for the SMU institution, USP Lewisburg, which we adjusted for inflation.

[55]GAO, *Bureau of Prisons: Improvements Needed in Bureau of Prisons' Monitoring and Evaluation of Impact of Segregated Housing,* GAO-13-429 (Washington, D.C.: May 1, 2013).

activation, its uncertainty regarding the number and security level of the inmates it plans to house there underscores the challenge of activating institutions without a comprehensive policy and without a schedule anchored in best practices, as discussed earlier in the report. If BOP had a policy in place to guide its activation of new institutions and a schedule that could account for different scenarios, it would be better positioned to determine more precisely the number and type of inmate it plans to house at Administrative USP Thomson and help ensure that the institution is activated within schedule estimates. BOP would also be better positioned to make adjustments to account for changes in resources, as well as variations in cost, while keeping within established time frames.

Conclusions

BOP's six new institutions will reduce crowding system-wide, but doing so has cost more and taken longer than BOP initially estimated because of internal and external challenges, many of which, according to BOP officials, are outside of BOP's control. Doing more to guide the aspects of the activation process over which BOP does have control could prevent similar schedule delays in future activations. In particular, by using the BOP annual budget justifications to clearly communicate to Congress the factors that might delay activation, like institution locations, DOJ could more effectively mitigate activation challenges and better meet the bureau's needs. Further, ensuring that the Central Office is analyzing staffing data at individual institutions in the activation process and developing effective strategies to mitigate staffing challenges would help expedite the activation process. In addition, by developing and implementing a comprehensive activation policy that incorporates the knowledge of staff with experience activating institutions, as well as the four characteristics of scheduling best practices, BOP would be better positioned to ensure that future activations are implemented in accordance with realistic cost and schedule commitments. While the success of new institution activations relies heavily on congressional direction regarding activation funding, BOP ultimately is responsible for the taxpayer dollars it spends on construction, acquisition, and activation of new institutions. Taking action to address challenges that BOP can control will help mitigate obstacles in ongoing and future activation of new institutions.

Recommendations for Executive Action

To ensure that the challenges that BOP faces activating new institutions are clearly conveyed to decision makers, we recommend that, in future activations, the Attorney General use DOJ's annual congressional budget justification for BOP to communicate to Congress factors that might delay activations, such as challenges hiring staff and placing inmates associated with the locations of new institutions.

To better address obstacles that occur during the activation process and to help ensure that institutions are activated within estimated timeframes, including those institutions that do not currently have inmates, such as Administrative USP Thomson and USP Yazoo City, we recommend that the Director of the Bureau of Prisons take the following three actions:

- direct the Central Office to analyze staffing data at individual institutions in the activation process to assess their progress toward reaching authorized staffing levels and use that assessment to develop effective, tailored strategies to mitigate those challenges;
- develop and implement a comprehensive activation policy that incorporates the knowledge of staff with experience activating institutions; and
- develop and implement an activation schedule that incorporates the four characteristics of scheduling best practices.

Agency Comments and Our Evaluation

We provided a draft of this report to DOJ for review and comment. DOJ provided written comments, which are reprinted in appendix IV, and technical comments, which we incorporated as appropriate. DOJ agreed with all four of the recommendations and outlined steps to address them. If fully implemented, these actions will address the intent of our recommendations.

- With respect to the first recommendation, DOJ agreed to use the annual congressional budget justification to communicate with Congress any factors that might affect schedules in future activations.

- Regarding the second recommendation, DOJ agreed that BOP's Central Office will analyze staffing data at individual institutions in the activation process to assess progress toward reaching authorized staffing levels and use that assessment to develop effective strategies to mitigate those challenges. DOJ stated that BOP's regional offices will monitor staffing levels and report to the Central Office quarterly. BOP's Central Office will provide oversight of staffing at activating institutions and will work to develop effective strategies, such as using recruitment incentives, when hiring challenges occur at those institutions.

- In response to the third recommendation, DOJ agreed to develop and implement a comprehensive activation policy that incorporates the knowledge of staff with experience activating institutions. DOJ stated that BOP will use knowledgeable staff to develop a new institution activation handbook. However, DOJ did not state what information would be included in this new institution activation handbook or how it would differ from the current activation handbook template. Ultimately, BOP should have a consistent policy that staff at institutions can use during the activation process to ensure that all future activations follow the same process.

- Finally, for the fourth recommendation, DOJ agreed to develop and implement an activation schedule that incorporates the four characteristics of scheduling best practices. DOJ stated that a template of this schedule will be included in the new institution activation handbook and will take into account the best practices outlined in GAO's *Schedule Assessment Guide.*

Further, DOJ commented that BOP cannot begin the activation process until Congress provides the necessary funding, which occurs over multiple years. DOJ stated that it cannot be held to activation estimates included in its annual budget requests when it does not receive such funding. As we note in the report, each of the institutions in the activation process has experienced schedule slippages due to delays in receiving congressionally directed activation funding, which is outside of BOP's control, as well as challenges associated with institutions' locations. We also note that institutions have experienced delays even after BOP has received multiple years of congressionally directed activation funding, which indicates that there is more that BOP could do to ensure that institutions are activated within schedule estimates. If BOP had a schedule that reflected best practices, it could revise its estimates, when warranted, for when activation would be completed. The ability to make such schedule revisions would allow BOP to adjust for the risks associated with funding delays and more accurately reflect the status of activation.

Finally, DOJ commented that Administrative USP Thomson, like every newly activated prison, will increase BOP's future operational costs. DOJ also stated that BOP's primary cost driver is the number of inmates, not the number of prisons. We agree that activating any new institution will consequently increase BOP's operational costs, and that this is not specific to Administrative USP Thomson. We also agree, and have previously reported, that the number of inmates entering the federal prison system is the primary driver of operational costs, rather than the number of institutions that BOP operates.[56] However, we believe it is important to note that the acquisition or construction any new institution, including Administrative USP Thomson, will incur costs to operate and maintain in the future.

As agreed with your offices, unless you publicly announce the contents of this report earlier, we plan no further distribution until 30 days from the report date. At that time, we will send copies to the Attorney General of the United States, appropriate congressional committees, and other interested parties. In addition, the report will be available at no charge on the GAO Web site at http://www.gao.gov.

If you or your staff have any questions about this report, please contact me at (202) 512-9627 or maurerd@gao.gov. Contact points for our Offices of Congressional Relations and Public Affairs may be found on the last page of this report. Key contributors to this report are listed in appendix V.

David C. Maurer
Director, Homeland Security and Justice Issues

---

[56]GAO-14-121.

List of Requesters

The Honorable Tom Coburn
Ranking Member
Committee on Homeland Security and Governmental Affairs
United States Senate

The Honorable Charles Grassley
Ranking Member
Committee on the Judiciary
United States Senate

The Honorable Bob Goodlatte
Chairman
Committee on the Judiciary
House of Representatives

The Honorable F. James Sensenbrenner
Chairman
Subcommittee on Crime, Terrorism, Homeland Security and
Investigations
Committee on the Judiciary
House of Representatives

Appendix I: Description of Schedule Slippages due to Delays in Receiving Congressionally Directed Activation Funding

Each of the Federal Bureau of Prisons' (BOP) institutions in the activation process has had schedule slippages due to delays in receiving congressionally directed activation funding.[1] Such delays can exacerbate existing staffing challenges related to recruitment and retention, as discussed in appendix II. None of the six institutions is at rated capacity—the number of inmates that a given institution can safely and securely house.

- **Federal Correctional Institution (FCI) Mendota.** BOP estimated in fiscal year 2008 that FCI Mendota would be fully activated by fiscal year 2010, but received congressionally directed activation funding in fiscal year 2010. As a result, BOP subsequently revised this estimate to fully activate FCI Mendota in fiscal year 2011. After BOP received a second year of congressionally directed activation funding for FCI Mendota in fiscal year 2012, BOP determined the FCI would accept its first inmate in February 2012 and accepted the first inmate that same month.[2] As of August 2014, FCI Mendota has not reached rated capacity—4 fiscal years after BOP's initial estimates—with 85 percent of its 1,152 beds occupied.
- **FCI Berlin.** BOP estimated in fiscal year 2008 that FCI Berlin would be fully activated by fiscal year 2010. However, BOP subsequently revised this estimate to fully activate FCI Berlin in fiscal year 2011 because it had not received congressionally directed activation funding. After BOP received congressionally directed activation funding for FCI Berlin in fiscal year 2012, BOP determined that the FCI would accept its first inmate in January 2013 and accepted the first inmate 1 month later, in February. BOP received congressionally directed activation funding for FCI Berlin in fiscal year 2013. As of August 2014, FCI Berlin has not reached rated capacity—4 fiscal years after BOP's initial estimate—with 83 percent of its total 1,152 beds occupied.

---

[1]Generally, either the annual appropriation act or the conference report accompanying BOP's annual appropriation act directs BOP to use S&E appropriations for activation activities at particular institutions. Conference report language that is incorporated by reference into an appropriations act becomes part of the public law. However, BOP generally follows directives contained in the conference report language even if not incorporated into the appropriations act. For the purpose of this report, we refer to the conference report language as "congressional direction" and the related funding as "congressionally directed activation funding."

[2]A specific activation date is determined by the activating institution and regional office staff primarily based on funding, staffing, and training needs.

- **FCI Aliceville.** BOP estimated in fiscal year 2008 that FCI Aliceville would be fully activated by fiscal year 2011. However, BOP subsequently revised this estimate to fully activate FCI Aliceville in fiscal year 2012 because it did not receive congressionally directed activation funding. After BOP received congressionally directed activation funding for FCI Aliceville in fiscal year 2012, BOP determined that the FCI would accept the first inmate in June 2013 and accepted the first inmate 1 month later, in July. BOP received congressionally directed activation funding for FCI Aliceville in fiscal year 2013. As of August 2014, FCI Aliceville has not reached rated capacity—3 fiscal years after BOP's initial estimate—with 77 percent of its total 1,536 beds occupied.
- **FCI Hazelton.** BOP estimated in fiscal year 2008 that FCI Hazelton would be fully activated by fiscal year 2012. However, BOP subsequently pushed back this estimate twice—once to fully activate FCI Hazelton in fiscal year 2013 and again to fully activate the institution in fiscal year 2014—because it had not received congressionally directed activation funding. After BOP received congressionally directed activation funding for FCI Hazelton in fiscal year 2013, it determined that the FCI would accept its first inmate in March 2014. BOP received congressionally directed activation funding for FCI Hazelton in fiscal year 2014. However, as of August 2014, the institution has not yet reached rated capacity—2 years after BOP's initial estimate—with about 27 percent of its 1,152 beds occupied because of a leaking roof that had to be fixed before inmates were housed there.
- **U.S. Penitentiary (USP) Yazoo City.** BOP estimated in fiscal year 2009 that USP Yazoo City would be fully activated by fiscal year 2013. However, BOP subsequently revised this estimate to fully activate USP Yazoo City in fiscal year 2014 because it had not received congressionally directed activation funding. BOP received congressionally directed activation funding in fiscal years 2013 and 2014. According to BOP, it has not completed activation of the institution because it was waiting for a congressional response to its spend plan relating to fiscal year 2014 funding. BOP received responses from the Senate and House Committees on Appropriations in April and May 2014, respectively, supporting BOP's plans to activate USP Yazoo City. As of August 2014, USP Yazoo City has not admitted any inmates.
- **Administrative USP Thomson.** BOP initially estimated that Administrative USP Thomson would be fully activated by fiscal year 2011. However, BOP subsequently revised this estimate to fully activate Administrative USP Thomson in fiscal year 2014 because it had not received congressionally directed activation funding in fiscal

year 2012 or 2013. BOP received conflicting congressional direction regarding activation funding for Administrative USP Thomson in the committee reports corresponding to the DOJ/BOP fiscal year 2014 annual appropriations act.[3] BOP subsequently included funding to activate that institution in its fiscal year 2014 spend plan, which was submitted to the Committees on Appropriations. BOP received responses from the Senate and House Committees on Appropriations in April and May 2014, respectively. However, those responses also included conflicting direction regarding activation funding for Administrative USP Thomson. As of August 2014, Administrative USP Thomson has not admitted any inmates.

---

[3]Section 4 of the Consolidated Appropriations Act, 2014, Pub. L. No. 113-76, § 4 128 Stat. 5, 7, referenced an explanatory statement regarding the act, printed in the House of Representatives section of the Congressional Record, 160 Cong. Rec. H475, H507 (Jan. 15, 2014). The explanatory statement, which was to have the same effect as if it were a joint explanatory statement of a committee of conference, stated that report language included in House Report 113-171 or Senate Report 113-78 that is not changed by the explanatory statement or the act is approved. House Report 113-171, at 47, stated "[t]he Committee continues to prioritize maintaining staff levels at institutions and the continuation of activation activities, as necessary, at the four institutions which received fiscal year 2013 activation funding. No funding is included for the activation of the Thomson, Illinois facility." However, Senate Report 113-78, at 79, stated "[t]he Committee fully funds the requests to activate prisons that currently sit empty or partially empty due to prior year budget constraints. These funds will complete the activation of a medium-security prison located in Berlin, New Hampshire, and a medium-security prison for female inmates in Aliceville, Alabama, and begin activations of a high-security prison in Yazoo, Mississippi, a medium-security prison in Hazelton, West Virginia, and a high-security prison in Thomson, Illinois."

Appendix II: Analysis of BOP's Human Resources Data

We analyzed data from the Office of Personnel Management's (OPM) human resources database, Enterprise Human Resources Integration (EHRI) Statistical Data Mart,[1] on staffing levels at the three institutions in our review that are partially activated and found that each faced obstacles hiring staff up to authorized levels (see table 4).[2] Specifically, although FCI Aliceville, FCI Berlin, and FCI Mendota are all partially activated, none has a full complement of staff, as demonstrated by the number of employees on board each fiscal year.[3] For example, FCI Berlin is authorized to fill 378 positions and has been staffing the institution since fiscal year 2010, even though BOP first received activation funds for that institution in fiscal year 2012, but it was only 67 percent staffed at the end of fiscal year 2013.

---

[1]EHRI is a collection of human resources, payroll, and training data that facilitates management of personnel in the federal government.

[2]We included three of the four partially activated institutions because the staffing data for FCI Hazelton included staff on board across the entire complex, rather than by individual institution. As a result, we could not calculate the number of employees staffed by fiscal year or the percent currently staffed for that particular institution. Additionally, we did not include data on Administrative U.S. Penitentiary (USP) Thomson or USP Yazoo City because BOP has not begun activating those institutions. According to BOP officials, Administrative USP Thomson had two employees on staff to maintain the institution. We were unable to determine the number of staff at USP Yazoo City because, as with FCI Hazelton, staffing data were by the entire Yazoo City complex. As a result, we could not calculate the number of employees staffed by fiscal year or the percentage currently staffed for that particular institution.

[3]Staff "on board" at an agency refers to personnel employed as of September 30 of the reporting period. Staff "hired" refers to new appointments that occur within the fiscal year.

Table 4: Staff On Board at Partially Activated Federal Bureau of Prisons' (BOP) Institutions from Fiscal Years 2010 through 2013

Institution	Number of employees on board by fiscal year				Number of authorized positions	Number of authorized positions unfilled in fiscal year 2013	Percentage staffed
	2010	2011	2012	2013			
Federal Correctional Institution (FCI) Aliceville			84	240	378	138	63
FCI Berlin	2	16	123	252	378	126	67
FCI Mendota	55	171	250	261	359	98	73

Source: GAO analysis of Office of Personnel Management (OPM) data. I GAO-14-709

Note: These data reflect the number of staff on board on September 30 of each fiscal year. We included three of the four partially activated institutions because the staffing data for FCI Hazelton included staff on board across the entire complex, rather than by the individual institution. As a result, we could not calculate the number of employees on board by fiscal year or the percentage currently staffed for that particular institution. Additionally, we did not include data on Administrative U.S. Penitentiary (USP) Thomson because BOP has not begun activating that institution. As of June 2014, Administrative USP Thomson had two employees on staff to maintain the institution. Further, we were unable to determine the number of staff at USP Yazoo City because, as with FCI Hazelton, staffing data were by the entire Yazoo City complex. As a result, we could not calculate the number of employees staffed by fiscal year or the percentage currently staffed for that particular institution.

Furthermore, our analysis of OPM data demonstrates that two of the three partially activated institutions have experienced increases in the number of staff they hire each fiscal year through fiscal year 2013, when institutions hired greater numbers of staff in each consecutive year although authorized positions remained unfilled (see table 5). As a result, these staffing challenges have implications for activating institutions because, as BOP officials told us, being able to receive additional inmates and thereby reach rated capacity relies, in part, on having enough staff to provide adequate security for those inmates.

Table 5: Staff Hired at Partially Activated Federal Bureau of Prisons' (BOP) Institutions from Fiscal Years 2010 through July 2014

Institution	Number of employees hired by fiscal year					Total employees hired
	2010	2011	2012	2013	2014	
Federal Correctional Institution (FCI) Aliceville	-	-	52	71	25	**148**
FCI Berlin	-	1	39	72	34	**146**
FCI Mendota	40	64	55	31	50	**240**

Source: GAO analysis of Office of Personnel Management (OPM) data and BOP personnel data. I GAO-14-709

Note: We included three of the four partially activated institutions because the staffing data for FCI Hazelton included staff on board across the entire complex, rather than by the individual institution. As a result, we could not calculate the number of employees hired by fiscal year for that institution. Additionally, we did not include data on Administrative U.S. Penitentiary (USP) Thomson because BOP has not yet begun activating that institution. As of June 2014, Administrative USP Thomson had two employees on staff to maintain the institution. Further we were unable to determine the number of staff at USP Yazoo City because, as with FCI Hazelton, staffing data were by the entire Yazoo City complex. As a result, we could not calculate the number of employees hired for that particular institution. We used Office of Personnel Management (OPM) data to report hires through the end of each fiscal year. To report the most current data on hires in fiscal year 2014, we relied on BOP to provide this information from its personnel database. BOP's data include hires that occurred between October 2013 and July 2014. We determined that these data are comparable to OPM's data and are reliable for the purposes of our report.

In addition to facing challenges recruiting qualified applicants, officials from two of the six institutions we visited reported that they faced challenges in retaining both new hires and experienced BOP staff that transferred from other BOP institutions. Officials said that BOP staff transfer to activating institutions to gain experience before receiving promotions elsewhere, so some staff do not stay in those new institutions over time. Further, officials from all of the institutions we visited noted that certain positions, such as those for medical staff, are particularly challenging to fill because, among other things, it is difficult to provide competitive salaries for those positions compared with what those staff could make in the private sector. Officials from BOP's Central Office also noted that recruiting medical staff, such as doctors and nurses, was a challenge system-wide, not just within the institutions undergoing activation. In fact, one of BOP's objectives in its strategic plan is to attract and retain competent health care professionals using a range of strategies, including recruitment and retention bonuses. Similarly, our analysis of OPM data demonstrates that partially activated institutions have had staff sever employment with BOP (see table 6). For instance, each year more staff have separated from employment at FCI Mendota than in the prior year, for a total of 40 employees—about 21 percent of its total hires—from fiscal years 2010 through 2013.[4] Additionally, according to data provided by BOP from its personnel database for fiscal year 2014—through July—an additional 11 employees separated from FCI Mendota.

Table 6: Staff Separations for Partially Activated Federal Bureau of Prisons' (BOP) Institutions from Fiscal Years 2010 through July 2014

Institution	Number of staff hired from fiscal years 2010 through July 2014	Number of staff separated from BOP from fiscal years 2010 through July 2014	Separations as a percentage of hired staff from fiscal years 2010 through July 2014
Federal Correctional Institution (FCI) Aliceville	148	30	20.3%
FCI Berlin	146	21	14.4
FCI Mendota	240	51	21.3

Source: GAO analysis of Office of Personnel Management (OPM) data and BOP personnel data. I GAO-14-709

Note: Separations include, among other things, voluntary and mandatory retirement, resignations, terminations, and death of hired or existing staff. We used EHRI data to report hires and separations through the end of each relevant fiscal year. To report the most current data on hires in fiscal year 2014, we relied on BOP to provide this information from its personnel database. BOP's data include hires that occurred between October 2013 and July 2014. We determined that these data are comparable to OPM's data and are reliable for the purposes of our report.

---

[4]These transfers may include existing BOP staff that transferred in and out of that institution during this time frame.

Appendix III: Analysis of BOP's Schedules against Best Practices

We determined that BOP's schedules for activating the six institutions in our review are not reliable based on our assessment of whether those schedules met best practices as outlined in our *Schedule Assessment Guide*.[1]

Purpose and Scope of the Schedule Guide

In May 2012, we issued GAO's *Schedule Assessment Guide* to provide guidance to auditors in evaluating government programs. According to that guide, the success of a program depends, in part, on having an integrated and reliable master schedule that defines when and how long work will occur and how each activity is related to the others. A schedule is necessary for government programs for many reasons. The program schedule provides not only a road map for systematic project execution, but also the means by which to gauge progress, identify and resolve potential problems, and promote accountability at all levels of the program. A schedule provides a time sequence for the duration of a program's activities and helps those involved understand both the dates for major milestones and the activities that drive the schedule. A program schedule is also a way to develop a budget that incorporates the time it will take to complete phases of the project. Moreover, the schedule is an essential basis for managing trade-offs among cost, schedule, and scope. Among other things, scheduling allows program management to decide between possible sequences of activities, determine the flexibility of the schedule according to available resources, predict the consequences of managerial action or inaction on events, and allocate contingency plans to mitigate risks. Moreover, an integrated and reliable schedule can show when major events are expected to occur as well as the completion dates for all activities leading up to them, which can help determine if the program's parameters are realistic and achievable.

Our research has identified 10 best practices associated with effective schedule estimating, which can be collapsed into four general characteristics:

- comprehensive,
- controlled,
- well constructed, and
- credible.

---

[1]GAO, *GAO Schedule Assessment Guide: Best Practices for Project Schedules*, GAO-12-120G (Washington, D.C.: May 2012).

After reviewing documentation BOP submitted for its activation schedule estimates and conducting interviews with BOP officials involved in activations, we determined that the documents used as schedules by the six activating institutions are not reliable.[2] Collectively, the six BOP institutions minimally met two of the four characteristics of a reliable schedule and did not meet the remaining two characteristics, as summarized in table 7. To arrive at this determination, we examined the extent to which each of BOP's six activating institutions adhered to each of the 10 best practices. We then assigned a corresponding score. We took the average score for all six institutions, by best practice, and collapsed the 10 best practices into the four characteristics to get an average that reflected an overall assessment by schedule characteristic.[3]

Table 7: Summary Assessment of the Federal Bureau of Prisons' (BOP) Schedule Estimates for Six Institutions Compared against Best Practices

Characteristic	Best practice related to schedules	Average assessment score for all six institutions per best practice	Overall assessment by schedule characteristic[a]
Comprehensive schedules include • all activities, as defined in the project's work breakdown structure, which defines work necessary to accomplish objectives; • the labor, materials, travel, facilities, equipment, and the like needed to do the work; • whether resources identified above will be available when needed; and • how long each activity will take, allowing for discrete progress measurement, with specific start and finish dates.	Schedule captures all activities.	2	Minimally met (score of 1.72[b])
	Schedule has resources assigned to all activities.	2	
	Schedule establishes the durations of all activities.	1.17	

[2]A schedule is considered reliable if the overall assessment ratings for each of the four characteristics are substantially or fully met. If any of the characteristics are not met, minimally met, or partially met, then the schedule cannot be considered reliable.

[3]We first scored each of the six institutions on the 10 best practices: not met equaled 1, minimally met equaled 2, partially met equaled 3, substantially met equaled 4, and met equaled 5. Then, we took the average of the institutions' ratings for each best practice to determine the average assessment score for all six institutions per best practice. We then took the average of the assessment scores per best practice within each schedule characteristic. The resulting average becomes the "overall assessment by schedule characteristic" using the same scoring categories: not met equaled 1.0 to 1.4, minimally met equaled 1.5 to 2.4, partially met equaled 2.5 to 3.4, substantially met equaled 3.5 to 4.4, and met equaled 4.5 to 5.0.

Characteristic	Best practice related to schedules	Average assessment score for all six institutions per best practice	Overall assessment by schedule characteristic[a]
Controlled schedules are • updated periodically by schedulers trained in critical path method scheduling;[c] • statused using actual progress and logic to realistically forecast dates for program activities; • compared against a documented baseline schedule to determine variances from the plan; • accompanied by a corresponding baseline document that explains the overall approach to the project, defines assumptions, and describes unique features of the schedule; and • subject to a process to manage changes to the baseline schedule.	Schedule is updated with actual progress and logic.	1.5	Minimally met (score of 1.83)
	Baseline schedule is maintained.	2.17	
Well-constructed schedules include • all activities, logically sequenced with predecessor and successor logic; • limited amounts of unusual or complicated logic techniques that are justified in the schedule documentation; • a critical path that determines which activities drive the project's earliest completion date; and • total float, or slack, that accurately determines the schedule's flexibility.[d]	Schedule shows the sequence of all activities.	1	Not met (score of 1.0)
	Schedule confirms that the critical path is valid.	1	
	Schedule ensures there is reasonable total float.	1	
Credible schedules include • the order of events necessary to achieve aggregated products or outcomes; • varying levels of activities, supporting activities, and subtasks; • key dates that can be used to present status updates to management; • a level of confidence in meeting a project's completion date based on data about risks and opportunities for the project; and • necessary schedule contingency and high priority risks based on conducting a robust schedule risk analysis.	Schedule can be verified that it is traceable horizontally and vertically.	1	Not met (score of 1.0)
	Schedule risk analysis conducted.	1	

Source: GAO analysis of BOP schedules. I GAO-14-709

[a]Met—BOP provided complete evidence that satisfies the entire criterion, substantially met—BOP provided evidence that satisfies a large portion of the criterion, partially met—BOP provided evidence that satisfies about half of the criterion, minimally met—BOP provided evidence that satisfies a small portion of the criterion, and not met—BOP provided no evidence that satisfies any of the criterion.

[b]We first scored each of the six institutions on the 10 best practices: not met equaled 1, minimally met equaled 2, partially met equaled 3, substantially met equaled 4, and met equaled 5. Then, we took the average of the institutions' ratings for each best practice to determine the average assessment score for all six institutions per best practice. We then took the average of the assessment scores per best practice within each schedule characteristic. The resulting average becomes the "overall

assessment by schedule characteristic" using the same scoring categories: not met equaled 1.0 to 1.4, minimally met equaled 1.5 to 2.4, partially met equaled 2.5 to 3.4, substantially met equaled 3.5 to 4.4, and met equaled 4.5 to 5.0.

[c]The critical path method for scheduling is a process used to identify the activities that cannot be delayed without delaying the end date of a program.

[d]Total float, or slack, is the amount of time by which a predecessor activity can slip before the delay affects the program's estimated finish date.

As summarized above, BOP's six activating institutions minimally met two of the four characteristics of a reliable schedule and did not meet the remaining two characteristics. Each of the sections below provides greater detail about where BOP's practices were deficient.

Comprehensive. We reviewed the activation handbooks and staffing timeline documents that each of the six institutions completed and found that they minimally met the requirements for a comprehensive schedule, as illustrated by table 8.

Table 8: Extent to Which Federal Bureau of Prisons' (BOP) Schedules Were Comprehensive

Characteristic	Characteristic description	Assessment
Comprehensive	A schedule should reflect all activities as defined in the program's work breakdown structure, including activities to be performed; the resources (e.g., labor, materials, and overhead) needed to do the work; and how long each activity will take.	Minimally met

Source: GAO analysis of BOP schedules. I GAO-14-709

To guide activation, BOP's Central Office provides each activating institution with a standard activation handbook template and general staffing timeline. With respect to the activation handbook template provided to activating institutions, this document contains some elements of a work breakdown structure, which is an important feature in a comprehensive schedule. In particular, the activation handbook template lists necessary tasks, organized by responsible departments or contractors. However, the activation handbook template provides the tasks, or activities, in the list in a general way, but none of the six institutions tailored the tasks to meet their specific requirements, which limits the bureau's ability to oversee all activation activities. Similarly, the activation handbook template does not fully include all work associated with each deliverable and does not identify the specific personnel within the department responsible for each activity—and none of the six institutions modified the template to provide this information. For example, the activation handbook template specifies that the Correctional Services department is responsible for coordinating with on-site project staff to evaluate all entrances, doors, locks, intercoms, cameras, and so forth. However, it does not provide additional detail about what is required as part of these evaluations, how these requirements might differ by institution, which specific staff should be executing or overseeing these activities, or what the costs associated with this activity might be. Two of the six institutions adapted the activation handbook template to provide detail on some resource costs associated with activation. In the case of FCI Berlin, that institution's activation handbook included details on the associated costs by department, such as Correctional Services, Food Services, or Medical Services, and the materials those departments would need to provide services to inmates, such as vaccines. However, FCI Berlin's activation handbook did not provide sufficient information about why the specific resources would be needed to keep the activation on schedule and the impact of not having the resources. Finally, none of the six institutions included any reference to project duration in its respective modified activation handbook. For example, the activation handbook template provided by BOP to activating institutions states that the Case Management Coordinator is responsible for establishing transfer arrangements for inmates and coordinating assignments for the transfers' work areas, but it does not provide an indication of how long the activity may take to complete. Without information about the estimated length of time required to complete each activity, management cannot accurately identify the staffing resources required to complete it, assess the progress of the activation process, or establish realistic dates for institution activation.

With respect to the general staffing timeline template BOP's Central Office provides, this document roughly identifies when particular staff resources are needed based on the anticipated activation date. For example, the general staffing timeline template specifies that 7 months prior to activation, the institution should hire the Warden, Executive Assistant, and Secretary within the Executive Staff department. However, the general staffing timeline template is based on the anticipated activation date rather than based on the activities each of these individuals would be doing—and none of the six institutions made modifications to elaborate on these activities. According to best practices for comprehensive schedules, resources, such as staff, should be assigned to particular activities in order to facilitate completion of these activities.

Because of these deficiencies, the information contained in each of the six institutions' activation handbooks and staffing timelines does not assist management in forecasting whether activities will be completed as scheduled or as budgeted. Further, these documents do not allow insight into the allocation of resources, increasing the likelihood that the activation process will not be completed as anticipated and limiting BOP's ability to ensure accountability for the total scope of work.

Controlled. The activation handbooks and staffing timeline templates that each of the six institutions modified minimally met the requirements for a controlled schedule, as illustrated in table 9.

Table 9: Extent to Which Federal Bureau of Prisons' (BOP) Schedules Were Controlled

Characteristic	Characteristic description	Assessment
Controlled	A schedule should be updated periodically using logic and actual progress to realistically forecast dates for program activities. A schedule narrative should accompany the updated schedule to provide decision makers and auditors a log of changes and their effect, if any, on the schedule time frame. The schedule narrative should contain key dates, a description of critical paths, and significant variances between planned and actual performance. This analysis is especially important for those variations that affect activities identified as being in a program's critical path and that can affect a scheduled completion date. A baseline schedule should be used to manage the program scope, the time period for accomplishing it, and the required resources.	Minimally met

Source: GAO analysis of BOP schedules. I GAO-14-709

Two of the activating institutions provided versions of BOP's activation handbook and staffing timeline templates that contained some indication that information on key dates and activities was updated at some point in time by the activating institutions. However, those activation handbook and staffing timeline templates modified by each institution did not indicate whether they had been updated at regular intervals, or that they reflected the actual status of the respective activations. For example, the activation handbook and staffing timeline templates modified by officials at FCI Aliceville that were used to guide that activation included handwritten dates for when specific steps in the activation process were expected to be completed, but these did not appear to be updated systematically or include an indication of when or if those activities had been completed. Further, none of the activating institutions' activation handbooks or staffing timelines included the status of key milestone dates, such as whether specific activities had been completed, or when the activation should be completed. In addition, none of the activating institutions used activation handbooks or staffing timelines that described the critical risks that the institution faced in meeting its goals for activation or contingencies if those risks were realized. As BOP officials have noted, meeting scheduled dates for activation is often dependent on receiving specific activation funding as planned, and, according to best practices for a controlled schedule, such risks should be documented to ensure reliability. Without regularly updating the schedule based on the current status of the activation at each respective institution, BOP is limited in its ability to monitor activation progress or make decisions on how to mitigate risk or allocate resources for activating institutions.

Well constructed. The activation handbooks and staffing timeline documents that each of the six institutions modified did not meet the requirements for a well-constructed schedule, as illustrated in table 10.

Table 10: Extent to Which Federal Bureau of Prisons' (BOP) Schedules Were Well Constructed

Characteristic	Characteristic description	Assessment
Well constructed	A schedule should be planned so that critical project dates can be met. To meet this objective, all activities should be logically sequenced—that is, listed in the order in which they are to be carried out. In particular, activities that must finish prior to the start of other activities (i.e., predecessor activities), as well as activities that cannot begin until other activities are completed (i.e., successor activities), should be identified. The establishment of a critical path between one activity and its successor is necessary for examining the effects of any activity slipping along this path. The calculation of a critical path determines which activities drive the project's earliest completion date. The schedule should also identify total float, or the amount of time a predecessor activity can slip, so that the schedule's flexibility can be accurately determined.	Not met

Source: GAO analysis of BOP schedules. I GAO-14-709

The activation handbook and staffing timeline templates modified by activating institutions did not always provide specific information regarding start and finish dates, durations, or sequencing of activation-related activities. For example, BOP's general staffing timeline template identifies the sequence in which staff should be hired, which is an important feature of a well-constructed schedule, but there is no sequencing of the activities listed in the activation handbook template. For example, the general staffing timeline specifies that within the Facilities department, the Communication Technician should be hired 7 months prior to activation, while the Facility Manager and Electrician and others should be hired 6 months prior to activation, but it does not provide contingencies if predecessor positions cannot be filled "on time" or describe the effects, if any, of filling positions out of sequence. Aside from staffing-related issues, the activation handbook template does not contain information on the order in which any of the activation tasks should occur. As a result, BOP does not have insight about the interdependencies between activities or the way in which early delays in some activities could affect activities later on as well as the overall activation completion date. Additionally, without identifying linkages between activities, BOP does not know the critical path of the activation process—that is, which activities can or cannot be delayed if the overall schedule is to be met. This prevents the agency from providing Congress with reliable timeline estimates or anticipated activation dates.

Credible. The activation handbook and staffing timeline templates that each of the six institutions modified did not meet the requirements for a credible schedule, as illustrated in table 11.

Table 11: Extent to Which Federal Bureau of Prisons' (BOP) Schedules Were Credible

Characteristic	Characteristic description	Assessment
Credible	A schedule should be horizontally and vertically integrated. A horizontally integrated schedule links products and outcomes with other associated sequenced activities, which helps verify that activities are arranged in the right order to achieve aggregated products or outcomes. A vertically integrated schedule ensures that the start and completion dates for activities are aligned with such dates on subsidiary schedules supporting tasks and subtasks. Data about risks and opportunities are used to predict a level of confidence in meeting the project's completion date. The level of necessary schedule contingency and high-priority risks and opportunities are identified by conducting a robust schedule risk analysis.	Not met

Source: GAO analysis of BOP schedules. I GAO-14-709

With respect to the best practice of vertically and horizontally aligning activities, two institutions adapted BOP's activation handbook template to insert targeted due dates for selected activities; however, neither identified subset activities or linked overall activities in any specific order. Without this vertical alignment, BOP is not positioned to ensure that subactivities are on track for an overall activity's completion. Similarly, without a clear sequencing of all activities, which is horizontal integration, BOP also is limited in the extent to which it can monitor overall progress toward activation. For risk assessment, neither the activation handbook template nor the staffing timeline contains a schedule risk analysis. Such an analysis typically focuses on key risks and how they affect the schedule's activities. Without a schedule risk analysis, the likelihood of the project's completion date or the activities or risks, such as funding details, most likely to delay activation cannot be determined.

The activation handbooks and general staffing timeline templates that BOP has developed and institutions have modified during activation are positive steps toward a baseline schedule that could be used to guide future institution activations, because they provide some level of detail regarding the activities required for activation. However, the activation handbook and general staffing timeline contain only limited information consistent with best practices and therefore cannot be used by management to reliably measure, monitor, or report on performance.

Appendix IV: Comments from the Department of Justice

U.S. Department of Justice

Washington, D.C. 20530

AUG 1 2 2014

Mr. David C. Maurer
Director, Homeland Security and Justice Issues
Government Accountability Office
441 G Street, NW
Washington, DC 20548

Dear Mr. Maurer:

Thank you for the opportunity to respond to the Government Accountability Office (GAO) report to congressional requesters entitled "Bureau of Prisons: Management of New Prison Activations Can Be Improved." The Department of Justice appreciates GAO's diligence in examining the Bureau of Prisons' (BOP) prison activation processes, and we thank you for the opportunity to review and discuss a previous draft of the report. While we note that GAO has addressed the majority of our concerns, the Department has several comments described below and has provided GAO with final technical comments under separate cover.

As the report's title suggests, most of the report focuses on BOP's activation processes generally. However, the report also addresses the question of why the Department purchased the Thomson Correctional Center from the state of Illinois and how the purchase affects system-wide costs.

The purchase of the Thomson Correctional Center was a demonstrably cost effective alternative to new prison construction that will reduce the 54 percent high security overcrowding situation in BOP facilities to 38 percent, significantly improving staff and inmate safety. The purchase of Thomson saved taxpayers over $200 million compared to the approximately $400 million which would be required to construct a similar facility.

GAO's report states that Thomson will increase BOP's operational costs in the future, as if to suggest Thomson is somehow different from BOP's other 120 facilities when it comes to incurring annual operating costs. *Any* prison system expansion increases future costs. The prison BOP activated immediately before Thomson increased annual operating costs, as will any prison BOP activates after Thomson. A more salient observation is this: *new prisons* are not BOP's primary cost driver, it is *new inmates*. That is why the Department is working on a variety of policy initiatives, such as sentencing reform, prisoner re-entry programs, and alternatives to incarceration, to address the prison population while maintaining public safety.

Mr. David C. Maurer   Page 2

In addition, we believe that GAO's statement that BOP is behind schedule in activating all six institutions is misleading. As its starting point, GAO uses time-to-activate estimates the Administration submitted with the Department's congressional budget requests for funding to construct or acquire the institutions. These estimates are assumptions based on timely funding. BOP cannot actually begin the activation process (hiring and training of staff, equipping and furnishing the institution, and gradually filling the institution with inmates), until Congress provides the requisite funding, which is a multi-year process. GAO does note that funding delays negatively impact BOP's ability to fully activate institutions. Realistically, however, the Department only can be held to activation estimates when congressional funding milestones are timely met.

GAO Recommendations

GAO offers the Department two recommendations. Our responses to these recommendations follow:

1. To ensure that the challenges that BOP faces activating new institutions are clearly conveyed to decision makers, we recommend that, in future activations, the Attorney General use DOJ's annual congressional budget justification for BOP to communicate to Congress factors that might delay activations, such as challenges hiring staff and placing inmates associated with the locations of new institutions.

   RESPONSE: The Department concurs with the recommendation.

   In future activations, the Department agrees to use the annual congressional budget justification to communicate with Congress any factors that might affect activation scheduling.

2. To better address obstacles that occur during the activation process and to help ensure that institutions are activated within estimated timeframes, including those institutions that do not currently have inmates, such as the Administrative USP Thomson and USP Yazoo City, we recommend that the Director of the Bureau of Prisons take the following three actions:

   - direct the Central Office to analyze staffing data at individual institutions in the activation process to assess progress toward reaching authorized staffing levels and use that assessment to develop effective strategies to mitigate those challenges;
   - develop and implement a comprehensive activation policy that incorporates the knowledge of staff with experience activating institutions; and
   - develop and implement an activation schedule that incorporates the four characteristics of scheduling best practices.

Mr. David C. Maurer   Page 3

RESPONSE: The Department concurs with the recommendation.

During the activation process, Regional Human Resource offices will monitor institution staffing levels and report to Central Office quarterly. If there are difficulties in filling positions, Central Office will explore the use of hiring flexibilities to include: relocation/retention/recruitment incentives, student loan repayment, annual leave credit, above the minimum rate appointments, age waivers, direct hire authority, or special salary rates. This oversight will continue until the institution is fully activated.

BOP will use knowledgeable staff to develop a comprehensive New Institution Activation Handbook. The enhanced handbook will include a comprehensive schedule template for the activation of newly constructed institutions along with specific guidance for activating Wardens.

For institutions constructed in the future, BOP will develop a comprehensive schedule for the activation of the institutions. A template of the schedule will be incorporated into the New Institution Activation Handbook. The schedule will take into account the best practices for project schedules described in the GAO Schedule Assessment Guide.

Thank you, again, for the opportunity to comment on this report. We look forward to working with GAO as we strive to improve our programs and further our mission.

Sincerely,

Lee J. Lofthus
Assistant Attorney General
    for Administration

Appendix V: GAO Contact and Staff Acknowledgments

GAO Contact	Dave Maurer, (202) 512-9627, maurerd@gao.gov
Staff Acknowledgments	In addition to the contact listed above, Joy Booth, Assistant Director; Pedro Almoguera; Billy Commons; Adam Couvillion; Emily Gunn; and Jan Montgomery made key contributions to this report. Also contributing to this report were Lorraine Ettaro, Susan Hsu, Elizabeth Kowalewski, Karen Richey, Rebecca Shea, and William Varettoni.

GAO's Mission	The Government Accountability Office, the audit, evaluation, and investigative arm of Congress, exists to support Congress in meeting its constitutional responsibilities and to help improve the performance and accountability of the federal government for the American people. GAO examines the use of public funds; evaluates federal programs and policies; and provides analyses, recommendations, and other assistance to help Congress make informed oversight, policy, and funding decisions. GAO's commitment to good government is reflected in its core values of accountability, integrity, and reliability.
Obtaining Copies of GAO Reports and Testimony	The fastest and easiest way to obtain copies of GAO documents at no cost is through GAO's website (http://www.gao.gov). Each weekday afternoon, GAO posts on its website newly released reports, testimony, and correspondence. To have GAO e-mail you a list of newly posted products, go to http://www.gao.gov and select "E-mail Updates."
Order by Phone	The price of each GAO publication reflects GAO's actual cost of production and distribution and depends on the number of pages in the publication and whether the publication is printed in color or black and white. Pricing and ordering information is posted on GAO's website, http://www.gao.gov/ordering.htm. Place orders by calling (202) 512-6000, toll free (866) 801-7077, or TDD (202) 512-2537. Orders may be paid for using American Express, Discover Card, MasterCard, Visa, check, or money order. Call for additional information.
Connect with GAO	Connect with GAO on Facebook, Flickr, Twitter, and YouTube. Subscribe to our RSS Feeds or E-mail Updates. Listen to our Podcasts. Visit GAO on the web at www.gao.gov.
To Report Fraud, Waste, and Abuse in Federal Programs	Contact: Website: http://www.gao.gov/fraudnet/fraudnet.htm E-mail: fraudnet@gao.gov Automated answering system: (800) 424-5454 or (202) 512-7470
Congressional Relations	Katherine Siggerud, Managing Director, siggerudk@gao.gov, (202) 512-4400, U.S. Government Accountability Office, 441 G Street NW, Room 7125, Washington, DC 20548
Public Affairs	Chuck Young, Managing Director, youngc1@gao.gov, (202) 512-4800 U.S. Government Accountability Office, 441 G Street NW, Room 7149 Washington, DC 20548

Please Print on Recycled Paper.